BIG IDEAS
MATH.
RED

Record and Practice Journal

BIG IDEAS LEARNING.

Erie, Pennsylvania

ISBN 13: 978-1-60840-034-8
ISBN 10: 1-60840-034-4

123456789-VLP-13 12 11 10 09

Contents

Contents

Chapter 1 · Fair Game Review

Order the integers from least to greatest.

1. $-9, 8, 0, 3, -7$

2. $-2, -4, 1, 2, -1$

3. $-11, -6, -8, 5, 9$

4. $4, 2, -5, 0, -7$

Use the graph to write an ordered pair corresponding to the point.

5. Point A

6. Point B

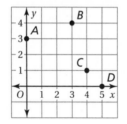

7. Point C

8. Point D

9. The table shows the lowest temperature recorded in January for five cities. Order the temperatures from least to greatest.

City	Boston	Nashville	Miami	Chicago	Dallas
Temperature (°F)	−12	−17	30	−27	4

Chapter 1 **Fair Game Review** (continued)

Evaluate the expression.

10. $2 + 1 \bullet 4^2 - 12 \div 3$

11. $8^2 \div 16 \bullet 2 - 5$

12. $7(9 - 3) + 6^2 \bullet 10 - 8$

13. $3 \bullet 5 - 10 + 9(2 + 1)^2$

14. $8(6 + 5) - (9^2 + 3) \div 7$

15. $5[3(12 - 8)] - 6 \bullet 8 + 2^2$

16. $4 + 4 + 5 \times 2 \times 5 + (3 + 3 + 3) \times 6 \times 6 + 2 + 2$

    a. Evaluate the expression.

    b. Rewrite the expression using what you know about order of operations. Then evaluate.

1.1 Integers and Absolute Value
For use with Activity 1.1

Essential Question   How are velocity and speed related?

On these two pages, you will investigate vertical motion (up or down).

- Speed tells how fast an object is moving, but does not tell the direction.
- Velocity tells how fast an object is moving and also tells the direction.

    If velocity is positive, the object is moving up.

    If velocity if negative, the object is moving down.

1   EXAMPLE: Falling Parachute

You are gliding to the ground wearing a parachute. The table shows your height at different times.

Time (seconds)	0	1	2	3
Height (feet)	45	30	15	0

a. How many feet do you move each second? _____

b. What is your speed? Give the units. _____

c. Is your velocity *positive* or *negative*? _____

d. What is your velocity? Give the units. _____

2   ACTIVITY: Rising Balloons

Work with a partner. The table shows the height of a group of balloons.

Time (seconds)	0	1	2	3
Height (feet)	0	4	8	12

a. How many feet do the balloons move each second? _____

b. What is the speed of the balloons? Give the units. _____

c. Is the velocity *positive* or *negative*? _____

d. What is the velocity? Give the units. _____

1.1 Integers and Absolute Value (continued)

3 ACTIVITY: Finding Speed and Velocity

Work with a partner. The table shows the height of a firework's parachute.

Time (seconds)	Height (feet)
0	480
1	360
2	240
3	120
4	0

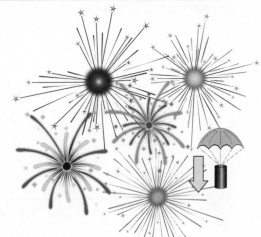

a. How many feet does the parachute move each second? _____

b. What is the speed of the parachute? Give the units. _____

c. Is the velocity *positive* or *negative*? _____

d. What is the velocity? Give the units. _____

Inductive Reasoning

4. Complete the table.

Velocity (feet per second)	−14	20	−2	0	25	−15
Speed (feet per second)						

5. Find two different velocities for which the speed is 16 feet per second.

6. Which number is greater: −4 or 3?

   Use a number line to explain your reasoning.

1.1 **Integers and Absolute Value** (continued)

7. One object has a velocity of −4 feet per second. Another object has a velocity of 3 feet per second. Which object has the greater speed? Explain your answer.

What Is Your Answer?

In this lesson, you will study **absolute value**. Here are some examples:

Absolute value of −16 = 16   Absolute value of 16 = 16

Absolute value of 0 = 0   Absolute value of −2 = 2

8. **IN YOUR OWN WORDS** How are velocity and speed related?

9. Which of the following is a true statement? Explain your reasoning.

   a. Absolute value of velocity = speed

   b. Absolute value of speed = velocity

Name _____ Date _____

1.1 Practice
For use after Lesson 1.1

Find the absolute value of the integer.

1. −1

2. −14

3. 0

4. 6

Complete the statement using <, >, or =.

5. 6 ___ $|-2|$

6. −7 ___ $|-8|$

7. $|-9|$ ___ 5

8. $|-2|$ ___ 2

Order the values from least to greatest.

9. 4, $|7|$, −1, $|-3|$, −4

10. $|2|$, −3, $|-5|$, −1, 6

11. $|-8|$, 0, −9, $|-7|$, −2

12. You download 12 new songs to your MP3 player. Then you delete 5 old songs. Write each amount as an integer.

13. The mantle layer of Earth begins about 70 kilometers underneath the surface. The layer called the outer core begins about 2970 kilometers underneath the surface.

    a. Write an integer for the position of each layer relative to the surface.

        Mantle layer _____   Outer core _____

    b. Which integer in part (a) is greater?

    c. Which integer in part (a) has the greater absolute value? How does this relate to the layer that has the greatest distance from the surface?

Name_____ Date_____

1.2 Adding Integers
For use with Activity 1.2

Essential Question Is the sum of two integers *positive*, *negative*, or *zero*? How can you tell?

1 **EXAMPLE:** Adding Integers with the Same Sign

Draw a picture to show how you use integer counters to find $-4 + (-3)$.

$-4 + (-3) =$ _____

2 **ACTIVITY:** Adding Integers with Different Signs

Work with a partner. Draw a picture to show how you use integer counters to find $-3 + 2$.

$-3 + 2 =$ _____

3 **EXAMPLE:** Adding Integers with Different Signs

Show how to use a number line to find $5 + (-3)$.

$5 + (-3) =$ _____

1.2 Adding Integers (continued)

4 ACTIVITY: Adding Integers with Different Signs

Work with a partner. Write the addition expression shown. Then find the sum.

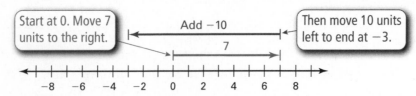

Start at 0. Move 7 units to the right.

Add −10

Then move 10 units left to end at −3.

7

Inductive Reasoning

Work with a partner. Use integer counters or a number line to complete the table.

	Exercise	Type of Sum	Sum	Sum: Positive, Negative, or Zero
1	**5.** $-4 + (-3)$			
2	**6.** $-3 + 2$			
3	**7.** $5 + (-3)$			
4	**8.** $7 + (-10)$			
	9. $2 + 4$			
	10. $-6 + (-2)$			
	11. $-5 + 9$			
	12. $15 + (-9)$			
	13. $-10 + 10$			
	14. $-6 + (-6)$			
	15. $12 + (-12)$			

1.2 **Adding Integers** (continued)

What Is Your Answer?

16. **IN YOUR OWN WORDS** Is the sum of two integers *positive*, *negative*, or *zero*? How can you tell?

17. Write a general rule for adding

    a. two integers with the same sign.

    b. two integers with different signs.

    c. an integer and its opposite.

Name _____ Date _____

1.2 Practice
For use after Lesson 1.2

Add.

1. $-9 + 2$

2. $5 + (-5)$

3. $-12 + (-6)$

4. $-10 + 19 + 5$

5. $-11 + (-20) + 9$

6. $-7 + 7 + (-8)$

Evaluate the expression when $a = 3$, $b = -6$, and $c = -2$.

7. $a + b$

8. $|b + c|$

9. $a + b + c$

10. $a + c + (-4)$

11. You have -30 points in a video game. You earn 57 points. What is your final score?

12. The table shows the change in your hair length over a year.

Month	January	February	August	September	December
Change in hair length (inches)	2	−1	3	−4	3

   a. What is the total change in your hair length at the end of the year?

   b. Is your hair longer in January or December? Explain your reasoning.

   c. When is your hair the longest? Explain your reasoning.

1.3 Subtracting Integers
For use with Activity 1.3

Essential Question How are adding integers and subtracting integers related?

1 EXAMPLE: Subtracting Integers

Draw a picture to show how you use integer counters to find $4 - 2$.

$4 - 2 =$ _____

2 ACTIVITY: Adding Integers

Work with a partner. Draw a picture to show how you use integer counters to find $4 + (-2)$.

$4 + (-2) =$ _____

3 EXAMPLE: Subtracting Integers

Show how to use a number line to find $-3 - 1$.

$-3 - 1 =$ _____

1.3 Subtracting Integers (continued)

4 ACTIVITY: Adding Integers

Work with a partner. Write the addition expression shown. Then find the sum.

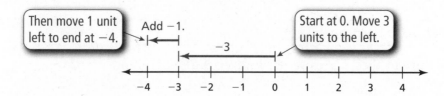

Inductive Reasoning

Work with a partner. Use integer counters or a number line to complete the table.

	Exercise	Operation: Add or Subtract	Answer
1	**5.** $4 - 2$		
2	**6.** $4 + (-2)$		
3	**7.** $-3 - 1$		
4	**8.** $-3 + (-1)$		
	9. $3 - 8$		
	10. $3 + (-8)$		
	11. $9 - 13$		
	12. $9 + (-13)$		
	13. $-6 - (-3)$		
	14. $-6 + 3$		
	15. $-5 - (-12)$		
	16. $-5 + 12$		

1.3 **Subtracting Integers** (continued)

What Is Your Answer?

17. **IN YOUR OWN WORDS** How are adding integers and subtracting integers related?

18. Write a general rule for subtracting integers.

Big Ideas Math Red **13**
Record and Practice Journal

1.3 Practice

For use after Lesson 1.3

Subtract.

1. $3 - 8$ **2.** $6 - (-7)$ **3.** $-10 - 9$ **4.** $-5 - (-4)$

Evaluate the expression.

5. $11 - (-2) + 14$ **6.** $-16 - (-12) + (-8)$ **7.** $6 - 17 - 4$

Evaluate the expression when $x = -4$, $y = -8$, and $z = 3$.

8. $6 - x$ **9.** $y - (-10)$ **10.** $-17 + z - x$ **11.** $|y - x|$

12. You begin a hike in Death Valley, California at an elevation of -86 meters. You hike to a point of elevation at 45 meters. What is your change in elevation?

13. You sell t-shirts for a fundraiser. It costs \$112 to have the t-shirts made. You make \$98 in sales. What is your profit?

14. The table shows the scores of six golfers. Find the range of the scores.

Golfer	1	2	3	4	5	6
Score	−5	−2	3	−3	1	−8

1.4 Multiplying Integers
For use with Activity 1.4

Essential Question Is the product of two integers *positive*, *negative*, or *zero*? How can you tell?

1 EXAMPLE: Multiplying Integers with the Same Sign

Use repeated addition to find 3 • 2.

Recall that multiplication is repeated addition. 3 • 2 means to add 3 groups of 2.

3 • 2 = _____

2 EXAMPLE: Multiplying Integers with Different Signs

Use repeated addition to find 3 • (−2).

3 • (−2) = _____

3 ACTIVITY: Multiplying Integers with Different Signs

Work with a partner. Use a table to find −3 • 2.

Describe the pattern in the table. Use the pattern to complete the table.

2 • 2 =		
1 • 2 =		
0 • 2 =		
−1 • 2 =		
−2 • 2 =		
−3 • 2 =		

−3 • 2 = _____

1.4 **Multiplying Integers** (continued)

4 **ACTIVITY:** Multiplying Integers with the Same Sign

Work with a partner. Use a table to find $-3 \cdot (-2)$.

Describe the pattern in the table. Use the pattern to complete the table.

-3	$\cdot$	3	$=$
-3	$\cdot$	2	$=$
-3	$\cdot$	1	$=$
-3	$\cdot$	0	$=$
-3	$\cdot$	-1	$=$
-3	$\cdot$	-2	$=$

$-3 \cdot (-2) =$ _____

Inductive Reasoning

Work with a partner. Complete the table.

	Exercise	Type of Product	Product	Product: Positive or Negative
1	**5.** $3 \cdot 2$			
2	**6.** $3 \cdot (-2)$			
3	**7.** $-3 \cdot 2$			
4	**8.** $-3 \cdot (-2)$			
	9. $6 \cdot 3$			
	10. $2 \cdot (-5)$			
	11. $-6 \cdot 5$			
	12. $-5 \cdot (-3)$			

1.4 Multiplying Integers (continued)

13. Write two integers whose product is 0.

What Is Your Answer?

14. IN YOUR OWN WORDS Is the product of two integers *positive*, *negative*, or *zero*? How can you tell?

15. Write a general rule for multiplying

    a. two integers with the same sign.

    b. two integers with different signs.

Name _____ Date _____

Multiply.

1. $8 \cdot 9$

2. $7(-7)$

3. $-10 \cdot 4$

4. $-5(-6)$

5. $12 \cdot (-1) \cdot (-2)$ **6.** $-10(-3)(-7)$

7. $-20 \cdot 0 \cdot (-4)$ **8.** $-4 \cdot 8 \cdot 3$

Evaluate the expression.

9. $(-8)^2$

10. -11^2

11. $9 \cdot (-5)^2$

12. $(-2)^3 \cdot (-6)$

13. You lose 5 points for every wrong answer in a trivia game. What integer represents the change in your points after answering 8 questions wrong?

14. A glacier is melting at a rate of 36 cubic miles each year. What integer represents the change in the glacier's volume over 4 years?

15. The value of a computer is given by the expression $2000 + (-200t)$, where t is the time in years.

a. Complete the table.

Time	1 year	2 years	3 years	4 years
Value				

b. Describe the change in the value of the computer for each year.

1.5 Dividing Integers
For use with Activity 1.5

Essential Question Is the quotient of two integers *positive*, *negative*, or *zero*? How can you tell?

1 EXAMPLE: Dividing Integers with Different Signs

Draw a picture to show how you use integer counters to find $-15 \div 3$.

$-15 \div 3 =$ _____

2 ACTIVITY: Rewriting a Product as a Quotient

Work with a partner. Rewrite the product $3 \cdot 4 = 12$ as a quotient in two different ways.

First Way

12 is equal to 3 groups of _____.

$12 \div 3 =$ _____

Second Way

12 is equal to 4 groups of _____.

$12 \div 4 =$ _____

3 EXAMPLE: Dividing Integers with Different Signs

Rewrite the product $-3 \cdot (-4) = 12$ as a quotient in two different ways.
What can you conclude?

First Way

Second Way

1.5 Dividing Integers (continued)

4 **EXAMPLE:** Dividing Negative Integers

Rewrite the product $3 \cdot (-4) = -12$ as a quotient in two different ways.
What can you conclude?

First way   *Second Way*

Inductive Reasoning

Work with a partner. Complete the table.

	Exercise	Type of Quotient	Quotient	Quotient: Positive, Negative, or Zero
1	**5.** $-15 \div 3$			
2	**6.** $12 \div 4$			
3	**7.** $12 \div (-3)$			
4	**8.** $-12 \div (-4)$			
	9. $-6 \div 2$			
	10. $-21 \div (-7)$			
	11. $10 \div (-2)$			
	12. $12 \div (-6)$			
	13. $0 \div (-15)$			
	14. $0 \div 4$			

1.5 **Dividing Integers** (continued)

What Is Your Answer?

15. **IN YOUR OWN WORDS** Is the quotient of two integers *positive*, *negative*, or *zero*? How can you tell?

16. Write a general rule for dividing

    a. two integers with the same sign.

    b. two integers with different signs.

Name _____ Date _____

1.5 Practice
For use after Lesson 1.5

Divide, if possible.

1. $3 \div (-1)$ **2.** $8 \div 2$ **3.** $-10 \div 5$ **4.** $-21 \div (-7)$

5. $\dfrac{48}{-6}$ **6.** $\dfrac{-13}{-13}$ **7.** $\dfrac{0}{3}$ **8.** $\dfrac{-55}{11}$

Evaluate the expression.

9. $-63 \div (-7) + 6$ **10.** $-5 - 12 \div 3$ **11.** $-8 \bullet 7 + 33 \div (-11)$

12. An online group loses 20 members over five months. What is the mean monthly change in the group membership?

13. The table shows the number of yards a football player runs in each quarter of a game. Find the mean number of yards the player runs per quarter.

Quarter	1	2	3	4
Yards	-2	14	-18	-6

14. The far north region of Alaska has an average temperature of $-22°F$ during the month of March. The interior region has an average temperature of $-2°F$ during the month of March. How many times colder is the far north region than the interior region during March?

1.6 The Coordinate Plane
For use with Activity 1.6

Essential Question How can you use ordered pairs to locate points in a coordinate plane?

1 EXAMPLE: Plotting Points in a Coordinate Plane

Plot the ordered pairs. Connect the points to make a picture. Color the picture when you are done.

1(4, 12)	**2**(9, 9)	**3**(12, 4)	**4**(12, –3)	**5**(10, –9)
6(9, –10)	**7**(7, –9)	**8**(2, –11)	**9**(–1, –11)	**10**(–3, –10)
11(–4, –8)	**12**(–11, –10)	**13**(–12, –9)	**14**(–11, –8)	**15**(–11, –6)
16(–12, –5)	**17**(–11, –4)	**18**(–4, –6)	**19**(–3, –3)	**20**(–4, 0)
21(–8, 2)	**22**(–8, 3)	**23**(–5, 8)	**24**(–1, 11)	

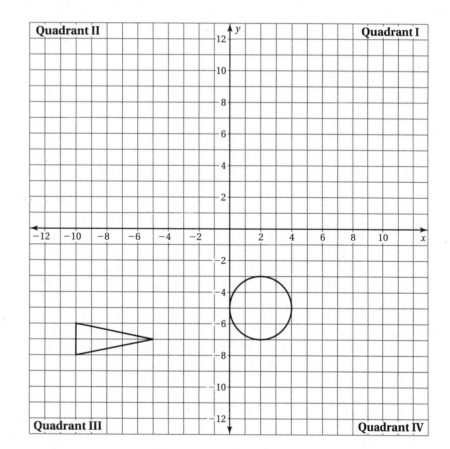

Name _____ Date _____

2 **ACTIVITY:** Plotting Points in a Coordinate Plane

Work with a partner.

Plot the ordered pairs. Connect the points to make a picture. Describe and color the picture when you are done.

1(6, 9)	**2**(4, 11)	**3**(2, 12)	**4**(0, 11)	**5**(−2, 9)
6(−6, 2)	**7**(−9, 1)	**8**(−11, −3)	**9**(−7, 0)	**10**(−5, −1)
11(−5, −5)	**12**(−4, −8)	**13**(−6, −10)	**14**(−3, −9)	**15**(−3, −10)
16(−4, −11)	**17**(−4, −12)	**18**(−3, −11)	**19**(−2, −12)	**20**(−2, −11)
21(−1, −12)	**22**(−1, −11)	**23**(−2, −10)	**24**(−2, −9)	**25**(1, −9)
26(2, −8)	**27**(2, −10)	**28**(1, −11)	**29**(1, −12)	**30**(2, −11)
31(3, −12)	**32**(3, −11)	**33**(4, −12)	**34**(4, −11)	**35**(3, −10)
36(3, −8)	**37**(4, −6)	**38**(6, 0)	**39**(9, −3)	**40**(9, −1)
41(8, 1)	**42**(5, 3)	**43**(3, 6)	**44**(3, 7)	**45**(4, 8)

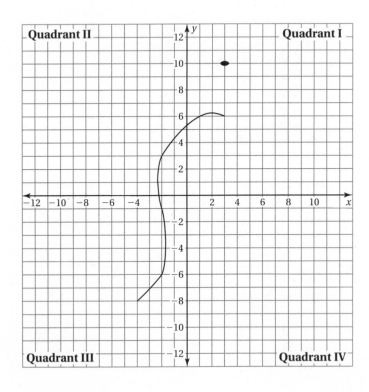

1.6 The Coordinate Plane (continued)

What Is Your Answer?

3. **IN YOUR OWN WORDS** How can you use ordered pairs to locate points in a coordinate plane?

4. Make up your own "dot-to-dot" picture. Use at least 20 points. Your picture should have at least two points in each quadrant.

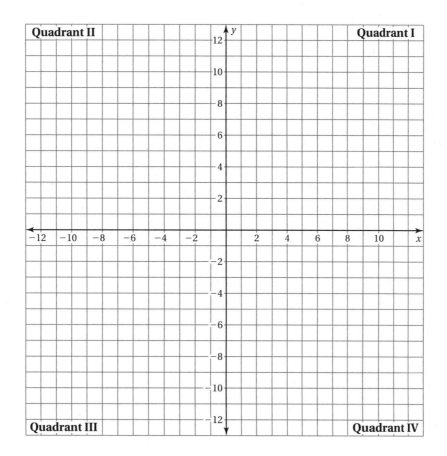

1.6 Practice
For use after Lesson 1.6

Plot the ordered pair in the coordinate plane. Describe the location of the point.

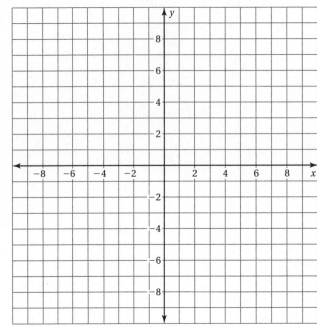

1. $A(8, 4)$

2. $B(-3, 5)$

3. $C(-2, -2)$

4. $D(4, -7)$

5. $E(-6, -5)$

6. $F(-9, 7)$

7. The coordinates of three vertices of a rectangle are shown in the figure. What are the coordinates of the fourth vertex?

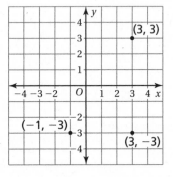

8. Your house is located at $(-4, 3)$, which is 4 blocks west and 3 blocks north of the center of town. To get from your house to the mall, you walk 7 blocks east and 4 blocks south.

    a. What ordered pair corresponds to the location of the mall?

    b. Is your house or the mall closer to the center of town? Explain.

Chapter 2 **Fair Game Review**

Write the decimal as a fraction.

1. 0.26

2. 0.79

3. 0.571

4. 0.846

Write the fraction as a decimal.

5. $\dfrac{3}{8}$

6. $\dfrac{4}{10}$

7. $\dfrac{11}{16}$

8. $\dfrac{17}{20}$

9. A quarterback completed 0.6 of his passes during a game. Write the decimal as a fraction.

Chapter 2 Fair Game Review (continued)

Evaluate the expression.

10. $\dfrac{1}{8} + \dfrac{1}{9}$

11. $\dfrac{2}{3} + \dfrac{9}{10}$

12. $\dfrac{7}{12} - \dfrac{1}{4}$

13. $\dfrac{6}{7} - \dfrac{4}{5}$

14. $\dfrac{5}{9} \cdot \dfrac{1}{3}$

15. $\dfrac{8}{15} \cdot \dfrac{3}{4}$

16. $\dfrac{7}{8} \div \dfrac{11}{16}$

17. $\dfrac{3}{10} \div \dfrac{2}{5}$

18. You have 8 cups of flour. A recipe calls for $\dfrac{2}{3}$ cup of flour. Another recipe calls for $\dfrac{1}{4}$ cup of flour. How much flour do you have left after making the recipes?

Name_____ Date_____

2.1 Rational Numbers
For use with Activity 2.1

Essential Question How can you use a number line to order rational numbers?

A **rational number** is a number that can be written as a ratio of two integers.

$$2 = \frac{2}{1} \qquad -3 = \frac{-3}{1} \qquad -\frac{1}{2} = \frac{-1}{2} \qquad 0.25 = \frac{1}{4}$$

1 ACTIVITY: Ordering Rational Numbers

Work in groups of five. Order the numbers from least to greatest.

a. $-0.5, 1.25, -\frac{1}{3}, 0.5, -\frac{5}{3}$

- Make a number line on the floor using masking tape and a marker.

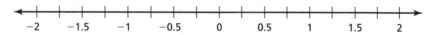

- Write the numbers on pieces of paper. Then each person should choose one piece of paper.

- Stand on the location of your number on the number line.

- Use your positions to order the numbers from least to greatest.

  The numbers from least to greatest are

  _____, _____, _____, _____, and _____.

b. $-\frac{7}{4}, 1.1, \frac{1}{2}, -\frac{1}{10}, -1.3$

c. $-\frac{1}{4}, 2.5, \frac{3}{4}, -1.7, -0.3$

d. $-1.4, -\frac{3}{5}, \frac{9}{2}, \frac{1}{4}, 0.9$

e. $\frac{9}{4}, 0.75, -\frac{5}{4}, -0.8, -1.1$

2.1 **Rational Numbers** (continued)

2 **ACTIVITY:** The Game of Math Card War

Preparation:

- Cut index cards to make 40 playing cards.*

- Write each number in the table on a card.

$\dfrac{3}{2}$	$\dfrac{3}{10}$	$-\dfrac{3}{4}$	-0.6	1.25	-0.15	$\dfrac{5}{4}$	$\dfrac{3}{5}$	-1.6	-0.3
$\dfrac{3}{20}$	$\dfrac{8}{5}$	-1.2	$\dfrac{19}{10}$	0.75	-1.5	$-\dfrac{6}{5}$	$-\dfrac{3}{5}$	1.2	0.3
1.5	1.9	-0.75	-0.4	$\dfrac{3}{4}$	$\dfrac{5}{4}$	-1.9	$\dfrac{2}{5}$	$-\dfrac{3}{20}$	$\dfrac{19}{10}$
$\dfrac{6}{5}$	$-\dfrac{3}{10}$	1.6	$-\dfrac{2}{5}$	0.6	0.15	$\dfrac{3}{2}$	-1.25	0.4	$-\dfrac{8}{5}$

To Play:

- Play with a partner.

- Deal 20 cards to each player face-down.

- Each player turns one card face-up. The player with the greater number wins. The winner collects both cards and places them at the bottom of his or her cards.

- Suppose there is a tie. Each player lays three cards face-down, then a new card face-up. The player with the greater of these new cards wins. The winner collects all ten cards and places them at the bottom of his or her cards.

- Continue playing until one player has all the cards. This player wins the game.

*Cut-outs are available in the back of the Record and Practice Journal.

2.1 **Rational Numbers** (continued)

What Is Your Answer?

3. **IN YOUR OWN WORDS** How can you use a number line to order rational numbers? Give an example.

The numbers are in order from least to greatest. Fill in the blank spaces with rational numbers.

4. $-\dfrac{1}{2}$, ▢ , $\dfrac{1}{3}$, ▢ , $\dfrac{7}{5}$, ▢

5. $-\dfrac{5}{2}$, ▢ , -1.9, ▢ , $-\dfrac{2}{3}$, ▢

6. $-\dfrac{1}{3}$, ▢ , -0.1, ▢ , $\dfrac{4}{5}$, ▢

7. -3.4, ▢ , -1.5, ▢ , 2.2, ▢

2.1 Practice
For use after Lesson 2.1

Write the rational number as a decimal.

1. $-\dfrac{9}{10}$

2. $-4\dfrac{2}{3}$

3. $1\dfrac{7}{16}$

Write the decimal as a fraction or mixed number in simplest form.

4. -0.84

5. 5.22

6. -1.716

Order the numbers from least to greatest.

7. $\dfrac{1}{5}, 0.1, -\dfrac{1}{2}, -0.25, 0.3$

8. $-1.6, \dfrac{5}{2}, -\dfrac{7}{8}, 0.9, -\dfrac{6}{5}$

9. $-\dfrac{2}{3}, \dfrac{5}{9}, 0.5, -1.3, -\dfrac{10}{3}$

10. Relative to ground level, a black garden ant digs $-20\dfrac{7}{9}$ feet and a red harvester ant digs $-20\dfrac{39}{50}$ feet. Which ant is closer to ground level?

11. The table shows the position of each runner relative to when the first place finisher crossed the finish line. Who finished in second place? Who finished in fifth place?

Runner	A	B	C	D	E	F
Meters	-1.264	$-\dfrac{5}{4}$	-1.015	-0.480	$-\dfrac{14}{25}$	$-\dfrac{13}{8}$

2.2 Adding and Subtracting Rational Numbers
For use with Activity 2.2

Essential Question How does adding and subtracting rational numbers compare with adding and subtracting integers?

---

1 ACTIVITY: Adding and Subtracting Rational Numbers

Work with a partner. Use a number line to find the sum or difference.

a. $2.7 + (-3.4)$

b. $\dfrac{3}{10} + \left(-\dfrac{9}{10}\right)$

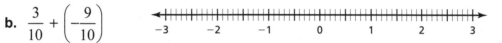

c. $-\dfrac{6}{10} - 1\dfrac{3}{10}$

d. $1.3 + (-3.4)$

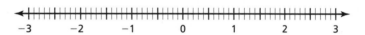

e. $-1.9 - 0.8$

2.2 **Adding and Subtracting Rational Numbers** (continued)

2 **ACTIVITY:** Adding and Subtracting Rational Numbers

Work with a partner. Write the numerical expression shown on the number line. Then find the sum or difference.

a.

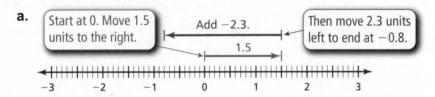

b.

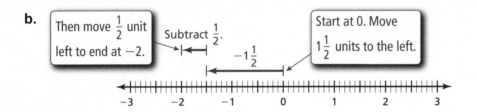

3 **ACTIVITY:** Financial Literacy

Work with a partner. The table shows the balance in a checkbook.

- Deposits and interest are amounts added to the account.

- Amounts shown in parentheses are taken from the account.

Date	Check #	Transaction	Amount	Balance
--	--	Previous Balance	--	100.00
1/02/2009	124	Groceries	(34.57)	
1/06/2009		Check deposit	875.50	
1/11/2009		ATM withdrawal	(40.00)	
1/14/2009	125	Electric company	(78.43)	
1/17/2009		Music store	(10.55)	
1/18/2009	126	Shoes	(47.21)	
1/20/2009		Check deposit	125.00	
1/21/2009		Interest	2.12	
1/22/2009	127	Cell phone	(59.99)	

2.2 Adding and Subtracting Rational Numbers (continued)

You can find the balance in the second row two different ways.

$$100.00 - 34.57 = 65.43 \qquad \text{Subtract 34.57 from 100.00.}$$

$$100.00 + (-34.57) = 65.43 \qquad \text{Add } -34.57 \text{ to } 100.00.$$

a. Complete the balance column of the table on the previous page.

b. How did you find the balance in the tenth row?

c. Use a different way to find the balance in part (b).

What Is Your Answer?

4. IN YOUR OWN WORDS How does adding and subtracting rational numbers compare with adding and subtracting integers? Give an example.

PUZZLE Find a path through the table so that the numbers add up to the sum. You can move horizontally or vertically.

5. Sum: $\dfrac{3}{4}$

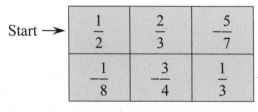

Start →

| $\dfrac{1}{2}$ | $\dfrac{2}{3}$ | $-\dfrac{5}{7}$ |
| $-\dfrac{1}{8}$ | $-\dfrac{3}{4}$ | $\dfrac{1}{3}$ |

← End

6. Sum: -0.07

Start →

| 2.43 | 1.75 | -0.98 |
| -1.09 | 3.47 | -4.88 |

← End

2.2 Practice
For use after Lesson 2.2

Add or subtract. Write fractions in simplest form.

1. $-\dfrac{4}{5} + \dfrac{3}{20}$

2. $-8 + \left(-\dfrac{6}{7}\right)$

3. $1\dfrac{2}{15} + \left(-3\dfrac{1}{2}\right)$

4. $-\dfrac{1}{6} - \dfrac{5}{12}$

5. $\dfrac{9}{10} - 3$

6. $5\dfrac{3}{4} - \left(-4\dfrac{5}{6}\right)$

7. $0.46 + (-0.642)$

8. $0.13 - 5.7$

9. $-2.57 - (-3.48)$

10. Tubs of ice cream are delivered to a store at a temperature of 36.7°F. The ice cream is stored in a −40°F freezer. When a tub is brought out of the freezer, its temperature is 22.2°F. Write the difference between the temperatures of the ice cream after the ice cream is in the freezer and before it is in the freezer.

11. Before a race, you start $4\dfrac{5}{8}$ feet behind your friend. At the halfway point, you are $3\dfrac{2}{3}$ feet ahead of your friend. What is the change in distance between you and your friend from the beginning of the race?

2.3 Multiplying and Dividing Rational Numbers
For use with Activity 2.3

Essential Question How can you use operations with rational numbers in a story?

1 EXAMPLE: Writing a Story

Write a story that uses addition, subtraction, multiplication, or division of rational numbers. Draw pictures for your story.

There are many possible stories. Here is an example.

Lauryn decides to earn some extra money. She sets up a lemonade stand. To get customers, she uses big plastic glasses and makes a sign saying "All you can drink for 50¢!"

24 Lemons	-$11.75
5 cups sugar	-$1.50
30 plastic glasses	-$1.50
18 sales ($0.50 each)	$9.00
PROFIT	-$5.75

Lauryn can see that her daily profit is negative. But, she decides to keep trying. After one week, she has the same profit each day.

Sunday	Monday	Tuesday	Wednesday	Thursday	Friday	Saturday
-$5.75	-$5.75	-$5.75	-$5.75	-$5.75	-$5.75	-$5.75

Lauryn is frustrated. Her daily profit for the first week is

$$7(-5.75) = (-5.75) + (-5.75) + (-5.75) + (-5.75) + (-5.75) + (-5.75) + (-5.75)$$
$$= -40.25.$$

She realizes that she has too many customers who are drinking a second and even a third glass of lemonade. So, she decides to try a new strategy. Soon, she has a customer. He buys a glass of lemonade and drinks it.

He hands the empty glass to Lauryn and says "*That was great. I'll have another glass.*" Today, Lauryn says "*That will be 50¢ more, please.*" The man says "*But, you only gave me one glass and the sign says 'All you can drink for 50¢!'*" Lauryn replies, "*One glass IS all you can drink for 50¢.*"

With her new sales strategy, Lauryn starts making a profit of $8.25 per day. Her profit for the second week is

$$7(8.25) = (8.25) + (8.25) + (8.25) + (8.25) + (8.25) + (8.25) + (8.25) = 57.75.$$

Her profit for the two weeks is $-40.25 + 57.75 = \$17.50$. So, Lauryn has made some money. She decides that she is on the right track.

2.3 **Multiplying and Dividing Rational Numbers** (continued)

2 **ACTIVITY:** Writing a Story

Work with a partner. Write a story that uses addition, subtraction, multiplication, or division of rational numbers.

- At least one of the numbers in the story has to be negative and *not* an integer.

- Draw pictures to help illustrate what is happening in the story.

- Include the solution of the problem in the story.

If you are having trouble thinking of a story, here are some common uses of negative numbers.

- A profit of –$15 is a loss of $15.

- An elevation of –100 feet is a depth of 100 feet below sea level.

- A gain of –5 yards in football is a loss of 5 yards.

- A score of –4 in golf is 4 strokes under par.

- A balance of –$25 in your checking account means the account is overdrawn by $25.

2.3 Multiplying and Dividing Rational Numbers (continued)

What Is Your Answer?

3. **IN YOUR OWN WORDS** How can you use operations with rational numbers in a story? You already used rational numbers in your story. Describe another use of a negative rational number in a story.

PUZZLE Read the cartoon. Fill in the blanks using 4s or 8s to make the equation true.

"Dear Mom, I'm in a hurry. To save time I won't be typing any 4's or 8's."

4. $\left(-\dfrac{1}{\boxed{}}\right) + \left(-\dfrac{1}{\boxed{}}\right) = -\dfrac{1}{\boxed{}}$

5. $\left(-\dfrac{1}{\boxed{}}\right) \times \left(-\dfrac{1}{\boxed{}}\right) = \dfrac{1}{6\boxed{}}$

6. $1.\boxed{} \times \left(-0.\boxed{}\right) = -1.\boxed{}\boxed{}$

7. $\left(-\dfrac{3}{\boxed{}}\right) \div \left(\dfrac{3}{\boxed{}}\right) = -\dfrac{1}{2}$

8. $-4.\boxed{} \div 2 = -2.\boxed{}$

2.3 Practice
For use after Lesson 2.3

Multiply or divide. Write fractions in simplest form.

1. $-\dfrac{8}{9}\left(-\dfrac{18}{25}\right)$

2. $-4\left(\dfrac{9}{16}\right)$

3. $-3\dfrac{3}{7} \times 2\dfrac{1}{2}$

4. $-\dfrac{2}{3} \div \dfrac{5}{9}$

5. $\dfrac{7}{13} \div (-2)$

6. $-5\dfrac{5}{8} \div \left(-4\dfrac{7}{12}\right)$

7. $-1.39 \times (-6.8)$

8. $-10 \div 0.22$

9. $-12.166 \div (-1.54)$

10. In a game of tug of war, your team changes $-1\dfrac{3}{10}$ feet in position every 10 seconds. What is your change in position after 30 seconds?

11. The table shows the change of gas prices over a month's time. What is the mean change?

Week	Change
1	−$0.06
2	+$0.10
3	−$0.08
4	+$0.02

2.4 Solving Equations Using Addition or Subtraction
For use with Activity 2.4

Essential Question How can you use inverse operations to solve an equation?

> **1** **EXAMPLE:** Using Addition to Solve an Equation

Use algebra tiles to model and solve $x - 3 = -4$.

Model the equation $x - 3 = -4$.
Draw a sketch of your tiles.

To get the green tile by itself, remove
the red tiles on the left side by adding
three yellow tiles to each side.

Remove the "zero pairs" from each side.
Draw a sketch of the remaining tiles.

The remaining tiles show the value of x.

$x = $ _____

> **2** **EXAMPLE:** Using Addition to Solve an Equation

Use algebra tiles to model and solve $-5 = n + 2$.

_____ $= n$ or $n = $ _____

2.4 **Solving Equations Using Addition or Subtraction** (continued)

3 **ACTIVITY:** Solving Equations Using Algebra Tiles

Work with a partner. Use algebra tiles to model and solve the equation.

a. $y + 10 = -5$ **b.** $p - 7 = -3$

c. $-15 = t - 5$ **d.** $8 = 12 + z$

4 **ACTIVITY:** Writing and Solving Equations

Work with a partner. Write an equation shown by the algebra tiles. Then solve.

a.

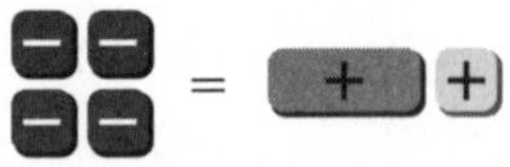

b.

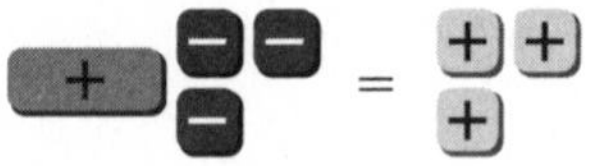

c.

d.

2.4 **Solving Equations Using Addition or Subtraction** (continued)

What Is Your Answer?

5. Decide whether the statement is *true* or *false*. Explain your reasoning.

  a. In an equation, any letter can be used as
  a variable.   _____

  b. The goal in solving an equation is to get the
  variable by itself.   _____

  c. In the solution, the variable always has to be
  on the left side of the equal sign.   _____

  d. If you add a number to one side, you should
  add it to the other side.   _____

6. IN YOUR OWN WORDS How can you use inverse operations to solve an
equation without algebra tiles? Give two examples.

7. What makes the cartoon funny?

"Dear Sir: Yesterday you said *x* = 2.
Today you are saying *x* = 3.
Please make up your mind."

8. The word *variable* comes from the word *vary*. For example,
the temperature in Maine varies a lot from winter to summer.
Write two other English sentences that use the word *vary*.

2.4 Practice
For use after Lesson 2.4

Solve the equation. Check your solution.

1. $y + 12 = -26$ **2.** $15 + c = -12$ **3.** $-16 = d + 21$

4. $n + 12.8 = -0.3$ **5.** $1\frac{1}{8} = g - 4\frac{2}{5}$ **6.** $-5.47 + k = -14.19$

Write the verbal sentence as an equation. Then solve.

7. 42 less than x is -50.   **8.** 32 is the sum of a number z and 9.

9. A clothing company makes a profit of $2.3 million. This is $4.1 million more than last year. What was the profit last year?

10. A drop on a wooden roller coaster is $-98\frac{1}{2}$ feet. A drop on a steel roller coaster is $100\frac{1}{4}$ feet lower than the drop on the wooden roller coaster. What is the drop on the steel roller coaster?

2.5 Solving Equations Using Multiplication or Division
For use with Activity 2.5

Essential Question How can you use multiplication or division to solve an equation?

1 ACTIVITY: Using Division to Solve an Equation

Work with a partner. Use algebra tiles to model and solve the equation.

   a. $3x = -12$

      Model the equation $3x = -12$. Draw a sketch of your tiles.

      Your goal is to get one green tile by itself.
      Because there are three green tiles, divide
      the red tiles into three equal groups.

      Keep one of the groups. This shows the value of x.
      Draw a sketch of the remaining tiles.

      $x =$ _____.

   b. $2k = -8$ **c.** $-15 = 3t$

   d. $-20 = 5m$ **e.** $4h = -16$

2.5 **Solving Equations Using Multiplication or Division** (continued)

2 ACTIVITY: Writing and Solving Equations

Work with a partner. Write an equation shown by the algebra tiles. Then solve.

a.

b.

c.

d.

3 ACTIVITY: The Game of Math Card War

Preparation:

- Cut index cards to make 40 playing cards.*

- Write each equation in the table on the next page on the card.

*Cut-outs are available in the back of the Record and Practice Journal.

Name_____ Date _____

2.5 **Solving Equations Using Multiplication or Division** (continued)

$-4x = -12$	$x - 1 = 1$	$x - 3 = 1$	$2x = -10$	$-9 = 9x$
$3 + x = -2$	$x = -2$	$-3x = -3$	$\dfrac{x}{-2} = -2$	$x = -6$
$6x = -36$	$-3x = -9$	$-7x = -14$	$x - 2 = 1$	$-1 = x + 5$
$x = -1$	$9x = -27$	$\dfrac{x}{3} = -1$	$-8 = -2x$	$x = 3$
$-7 = -1 + x$	$x = -5$	$-10 = 10x$	$x = -4$	$-2 = -3 + x$
$-20 = 10x$	$x + 9 = 8$	$-16 = 8x$	$x = 2$	$x + 13 = 11$
$x = -3$	$-8 = 2x$	$x = 1$	$\dfrac{x}{2} = -2$	$-4 + x = -2$
$\dfrac{x}{5} = -1$	$-6 = x - 3$	$x = 4$	$x + 6 = 2$	$x - 5 = -4$

To Play:

- Play with a partner. Deal 20 cards to each player face-down.

- Each player turns one card face-up. The player with the greater solution wins. The winner collects both cards and places them at the bottom of his or her cards.

- Suppose there is a tie. Each player lays three cards face-down, then a new card face-up. The player with the greater solution of these new cards wins. The winner collects all ten cards, and places them at the bottom of his or her cards.

- Continue playing until one player has all the cards. This player wins the game.

What Is Your Answer?

4. **IN YOUR OWN WORDS** How can you use multiplication or division to solve an equation without using algebra tiles? Give two examples.

Name _____ Date _____

Solve the equation. Check your solution.

1. $\dfrac{d}{5} = -6$

2. $8x = -6$

3. $-15 = \dfrac{z}{-2}$

4. $3.2n = -0.8$

5. $-\dfrac{3}{10}h = 15$

6. $-1.1k = -1.21$

Write the verbal sentence as an equation. Then solve.

7. A number divided by –8 is 7.

8. The product of –12 and a number is 60.

9. You earn $0.85 for every cup of hot chocolate you sell. How many cups do you need to sell to earn $55.25?

10. The price of a satellite radio at Store A is $\dfrac{29}{30}$ the price at Store B. The price at Store A is $150.80.

    a. Write and solve an equation to find the price of the satellite radio at Store B.

    b. How much do you save by buying the satellite radio at Store A?

2.6 Solving Two-Step Equations
For use with Activity 2.6

Essential Question In a two-step equation, which step should you do first?

---

1 **EXAMPLE:** Solving a Two-Step Equation

Use algebra tiles to model and solve $2x - 3 = -5$.

Model the equation $2x - 3 = -5$.
Draw a sketch of your tiles.

Remove the three red tiles on the left side by
adding _____ yellow tiles to each side.

Because there are two green tiles, divide the
red tiles into _____ equal groups.

Keep one of the groups. This shows the value of x.
Draw a sketch of the remaining tiles.

$x =$ _____.

---

2 **EXAMPLE:** The Math Behind the Tiles

Solve $2x - 3 = -5$ without using algebra tiles. Describe each step. Which step is first, adding 3 to each side or dividing each side by 2?

$x =$ _____. The first step is _____.

2.6 Solving Two-Step Equations (continued)

3 ACTIVITY: Solving Equations Using Algebra Tiles

Work with a partner.

- **Write an equation shown by the algebra tiles.**
- **Use algebra tiles to model and solve the equation.**
- **Check your answer by solving the equation without using algebra tiles.**

a.

b.

4 ACTIVITY: Working Backwards

Work with a partner.

a. Your friend pauses a video game to get a drink. You continue the game. You double the score by saving a princess. Then you lose 75 points because you do not collect the treasure. You finish the game with –25 points. How many points did you start with?

One way to solve the problem is to work backwards. To do this, start with the end result and retrace the events.

You started the game with _____ points.

2.6 **Solving Two-Step Equations** (continued)

b. You triple your account balance by making a deposit. Then you withdraw $127.32 to buy groceries. Your account is now overdrawn by $10.56. By working backwards, find your account balance before you made the deposit.

What Is Your Answer?

5. IN YOUR OWN WORDS In a two-step equation, which step should you do first? Give four examples.

6. Solve the equation $2x - 75 = -25$. How do your steps compare with the strategy of working backwards in Activity 4?

2.6 Practice
For use after Lesson 2.6

Solve the equation. Check your solution.

1. $3a - 5 = -14$

2. $10 = -2c + 22$

3. $18 = -5b - 17$

4. $-12 = -8z + 12$

5. $1.3n - 0.03 = -9$

6. $-\dfrac{5}{11}h + \dfrac{7}{9} = \dfrac{2}{9}$

7. It costs $34.95 to rent a jet ski for four hours plus $15.75 for each additional hour. You have $100. Can you rent the jet ski for 8 hours? Explain.

8. The length of a rectangle is 3 meters less than twice its width.

   a. Write an equation to find the length of the rectangle.

   b. The length of the rectangle is 11 meters. What is the width of the rectangle?

Chapter 3 Fair Game Review

Simplify.

1. $\dfrac{3}{18}$

2. $\dfrac{4}{6}$

3. $\dfrac{12}{60}$

4. $\dfrac{14}{28}$

5. $\dfrac{16}{36}$

6. $\dfrac{40}{50}$

Are the fractions equivalent?

7. $\dfrac{3}{8} \overset{?}{=} \dfrac{6}{11}$

8. $\dfrac{4}{10} \overset{?}{=} \dfrac{16}{40}$

9. $\dfrac{22}{32} \overset{?}{=} \dfrac{11}{16}$

10. $\dfrac{63}{72} \overset{?}{=} \dfrac{7}{9}$

11. You see 58 birds while on a bird watching tour. Of those birds, you see 12 hawks. Write and simplify the fraction of hawks you see.

Name _____ Date _____

Convert.

12. 12 feet = _____ yards

13. 28 quarts = _____ gallons

14. 48 inches = _____ feet

15. 10,000 pounds = _____ tons

16. 9 pints = _____ cups

17. 80 pounds = _____ ounces

18. 5 yards = _____ inches

19. 28 ounces = _____ pounds

20. You buy three gallons of fruit punch for a party. How many cups will that serve?

3.1 Ratios and Rates
For use with Activity 3.1

Essential Question How do rates help you describe real-life problems?

1 ACTIVITY: Finding Reasonable Rates

Work with a partner.

a. Match each description with a verbal rate.

b. Match each verbal rate with a numerical rate.

c. Give a reasonable numerical rate for each description.
Then give an unreasonable rate.

Description	Verbal Rate	Numerical Rate	
Your pay rate for washing cars	inches per month	$\dfrac{\boxed{}\ \text{m}}{\text{sec}}$;	$\dfrac{\boxed{}\ \text{m}}{\text{sec}}$
The average rainfall in a rain forest	pounds per acre	$\dfrac{\boxed{}\ \text{people}}{\text{yr}}$;	$\dfrac{\boxed{}\ \text{people}}{\text{yr}}$
Your average driving rate along an interstate	meters per second	$\dfrac{\boxed{}\ \text{lb}}{\text{acre}}$;	$\dfrac{\boxed{}\ \text{lb}}{\text{acre}}$
The growth rate for the length of a baby alligator	people per year	$\dfrac{\boxed{}\ \text{mi}}{\text{h}}$;	$\dfrac{\boxed{}\ \text{mi}}{\text{h}}$
Your running rate in a 100-meter dash	dollars per hour	$\dfrac{\boxed{}\ \text{in.}}{\text{yr}}$;	$\dfrac{\boxed{}\ \text{in.}}{\text{yr}}$
The population growth rate of a large city	dollars per year	$\dfrac{\boxed{}\ \text{in.}}{\text{mo}}$;	$\dfrac{\boxed{}\ \text{in.}}{\text{mo}}$
The average pay rate for a professional athlete	miles per hour	$\dfrac{\$\ \boxed{}}{\text{h}}$;	$\dfrac{\$\ \boxed{}}{\text{h}}$
The fertilization rate for an apple orchard	inches per year	$\dfrac{\$\ \boxed{}}{\text{yr}}$;	$\dfrac{\$\ \boxed{}}{\text{yr}}$

3.1 Ratios and Rates (continued)

2 ACTIVITY: Unit Analysis

Work with a partner. Some real-life problems involve the product of an amount and a rate. Find each product. List the units.

a. $6 \text{ h} \times \dfrac{\$12}{\text{h}}$

b. $6 \text{ mo} \times \dfrac{\$700}{\text{mo}}$

c. $10 \text{ gal} \times \dfrac{22 \text{ mi}}{\text{gal}}$

d. $9 \text{ lb} \times \dfrac{\$3}{\text{lb}}$

e. $13 \text{ min} \times \dfrac{60 \text{ sec}}{\text{min}}$

3 ACTIVITY: Writing a Story

Work with a partner.

- Think of a story that compares two different rates.
- Write the story.
- Draw pictures for the story.

3.1 **Ratios and Rates** (continued)

What Is Your Answer?

4. **RESEARCH** Use newspapers, the Internet, or magazines to find examples of salaries. Try to find examples of each of the following ways to write salaries.

   a. dollars per hour   **b.** dollars per month   **c.** dollars per year

5. **IN YOUR OWN WORDS** How do rates help you describe real-life problems? Give two examples.

6. To estimate the annual salary for a given hourly pay rate, multiply by 2 and insert "000" at the end. **Sample:** $10 per hour is about $20,000 per year.

   a. Explain why this works. Assume the person is working 40 hours a week.

   b. Estimate the annual salary for an hourly pay rate of $8 per hour.

   c. You earn $1 million per month. What is your annual salary?

   "We had someone apply for the job. He says he would like $1 million a month, but will settle for $8 an hour."

   d. Why is the cartoon funny?

3.1 Practice
For use after Lesson 3.1

Write the ratio as a fraction in simplest form.

1. 8 to 14

2. 36 even : 12 odd

3. 42 vanilla to 48 chocolate

Find the unit rate.

4. $2.50 for 5 ounces

5. 15 degrees in 2 hours

6. 183 miles in 3 hours

Use the table to find the rate.

7.

Boxes	0	1	2	3
Pounds	0	30	60	90

8.

Notebooks	0	5	10	15
Dollars	0	9.45	18.90	28.35

9. A laser printer prints 360 pages in 30 minutes. What is the printing rate in pages per minute?

10. A clothing store sells four shirts for $60.00. The next week, the store runs a special that is buy three shirts for $19.50 each, get the fourth free. Which is the better buy?

11. You create 15 centerpieces for a party in 5 hours.

a. What is the unit rate?

b. How long will it take you to make 42 centerpieces?

Name_____ Date _____

3.2 Slope
For use with Activity 3.2

Essential Question How can you compare two rates graphically?

---

1 **ACTIVITY:** Comparing Unit Rates

Work with a partner. The table shows the maximum speeds of several animals.

    a. Find the missing speeds. Round your answers to the nearest tenth.

    b. Which animal is fastest? Which animal is slowest?

    c. Explain how you convert between the two units of speed.

Animal	Speed (miles per hour)	Speed (feet per second)
Antelope	61.0	
Black Mamba Snake		29.3
Cheetah		102.6
Chicken		13.2
Coyote	43.0	
Domestic Pig		16.0
Elephant		36.6
Elk		66.0
Giant Tortoise	0.2	
Giraffe	32.0	
Gray Fox		61.6
Greyhound	39.4	
Grizzly Bear		44.0
Human		41.0
Hyena	40.0	
Jackal	35.0	
Lion		73.3
Peregrine Falcon	200.0	
Quarter Horse	47.5	
Spider		1.76
Squirrel	12.0	
Thomson's Gazelle	50.0	
Three-Toed Sloth		0.2
Tuna	47.0	

3.2 **Slope** (continued)

2 **ACTIVITY: Comparing Two Rates Graphically**

Work with a partner. A cheetah and a Thomson's gazelle are running at constant speeds.

   a. Find the missing distances.

	Cheetah	Gazelle
Time (seconds)	Distance (feet)	Distance (feet)
0	0	0
1	102.6	
2		
3		
4		
5		
6		
7		

   b. Use the table to complete the line graph for each animal.

   c. Which graph is steeper? The speed of which animal is greater?

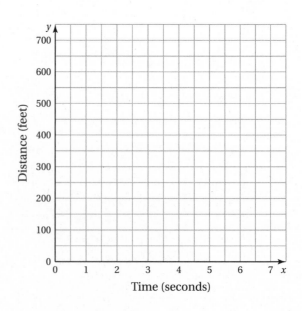

3.2 **Slope** (continued)

What Is Your Answer?

3. **IN YOUR OWN WORDS** How can you compare two rates graphically? Explain your reasoning. Give some examples with your answer.

4. Choose 10 animals from Activity 1.

   a. Make a table for each animal similar to the table in Activity 2.

   b. Sketch a graph of the distances for each animal.

   c. Compare the steepness of the 10 graphs. What can you conclude?

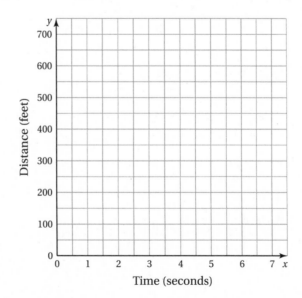

Name _____ Date _____

Find the slope of the line.

1.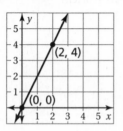

2.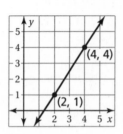

3.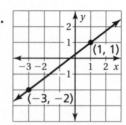

Graph the data. Then find the slope of the line through the points.

4.

Minutes, x	0	1	3	5
Pages, y	0	1.5	4.5	7.5

5.

Miles, x	0	1	2	3
Calories, y	0	135	270	405

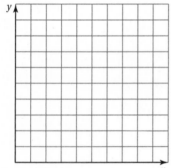

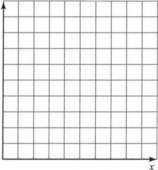

6. By law, the maximum slope of a wheelchair ramp is $\dfrac{1}{12}$.

    a. A ramp is designed that is 4 feet high and has a horizontal length of 50 feet. Does this ramp meet the law? Explain.

    b. What could be adjusted on an unacceptable ramp so that it meets the law?

3.3 Proportions
For use with Activity 3.3

Essential Question How can proportions help you decide when things are "fair"?

1 ACTIVITY: Determining Proportions

Work with a partner. Tell whether the two ratios are equivalent. If they are not equivalent, change the second day to make the ratios equivalent. Explain your reasoning.

a. On the first day, you pay $5 for 2 boxes of popcorn. The next day, you pay $7.50 for 3 boxes.

First Day

$$\frac{\$5.00}{\$7.50} \overset{?}{=} \frac{2 \text{ boxes}}{3 \text{ boxes}}$$

Next Day

b. On the first day, it takes you 3 hours to drive 135 miles. The next day, it takes you 5 hours to drive 200 miles.

First Day

$$\frac{3 \text{ h}}{5 \text{ h}} \overset{?}{=} \frac{135 \text{ mi}}{200 \text{ mi}}$$

Next Day

c. On the first day, you walk 4 miles and burn 300 calories. The next day, you walk 3 miles and burn 225 calories.

First Day

$$\frac{4 \text{ mi}}{3 \text{ mi}} \overset{?}{=} \frac{300 \text{ cal}}{225 \text{ cal}}$$

Next Day

d. On the first day, you download 5 songs and pay $2.25. The next day, you download 4 songs and pay $2.00.

First Day

$$\frac{5 \text{ songs}}{4 \text{ songs}} \overset{?}{=} \frac{\$2.25}{\$2.00}$$

Next Day

3.3 **Proportions** (continued)

---

2 **ACTIVITY:** Checking a Proportion

Work with a partner.

    a. It is said that "one year in a dog's life is equivalent to seven years in a human's life." Explain why Newton thinks he has a score of 105 points. Did he solve the proportion correctly?

$$\frac{1 \text{ year}}{7 \text{ years}} \overset{?}{=} \frac{15 \text{ points}}{105 \text{ points}}$$

"I got 15 on my online test. That's 105 in dog points! Isn't that an A+?"

    b. If Newton thinks his score is 98 points, how many points does he actually have? Explain your reasoning.

---

3 **ACTIVITY:** Determining Fairness

Work with a partner. Write a ratio for each sentence. If they are equal, then the answer is "It is fair." If they are not equal, then the answer is "It is not fair." Explain your reasoning.

    a.

| You pay $184 for 2 tickets to a concert. | **&** | I pay $266 for 3 tickets to the same concert. |

➡ **Is this fair?**

3.3 **Proportions** (continued)

b.

| You get 75 points for answering 15 questions correctly. | **&** | I get 70 points for answering 14 questions correctly. |

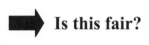 **Is this fair?**

c.

| You trade 24 football cards for 15 baseball cards. | **&** | I trade 20 football cards for 32 baseball cards. |

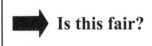 **Is this fair?**

What Is Your Answer?

4. Find a recipe for something you like to eat. Then show how two of the ingredient amounts are proportional when you double or triple the recipe.

5. IN YOUR OWN WORDS How can proportions help you decide when things are "fair?" Give an example.

3.3 Practice
For use after Lesson 3.3

Tell whether the ratios form a proportion.

1. $\dfrac{1}{5}, \dfrac{5}{15}$
2. $\dfrac{2}{3}, \dfrac{12}{18}$
3. $\dfrac{15}{2}, \dfrac{4}{30}$
4. $\dfrac{56}{21}, \dfrac{8}{3}$

5. $\dfrac{5}{8}, \dfrac{62.5}{100}$
6. $\dfrac{17}{20}, \dfrac{90.1}{106}$
7. $\dfrac{3.2}{4}, \dfrac{16}{24}$
8. $\dfrac{34}{50}, \dfrac{6.8}{10}$

Tell whether the two rates form a proportion.

9. 28 points in 3 games;
   112 points in 12 games

10. 32 notes in 4 measures;
    12 notes in 2 measures

11. You can type 105 words in two minutes. Your friend can type 210 words in four minutes. Are these rates proportional? Explain.

12. You make punch for a party. The ratio of ginger ale to fruit juice is 8 cups to 3 cups. You decide to add 4 more cups of ginger ale. How many more cups of fruit juice do you need to add to keep the correct ratio? Explain.

3.4 Writing Proportions
For use with Activity 3.4

Essential Question How can you write a proportion that solves a problem in real life?

---

1 ACTIVITY: Writing Proportions

Work with a partner. A rough rule for finding the correct bat length is "The bat length should be half of the batter's height." So, a 62-inch tall batter uses a bat that is 31 inches long. Write a proportion to find the bat length for each given batter height.

   a. 58 inches   **b.** 60 inches   **c.** 64 inches

---

2 ACTIVITY: Bat Lengths

Work with a partner. Here is a more accurate table for determining the bat length for a batter. Find all of the batter heights for which the rough rule in Activity 1 is exact.

	Height of Batter (inches)							
Weight of Batter (pounds)	**45–48**	**49–52**	**53–56**	**57–60**	**61–64**	**65–68**	**69–72**	**Over 72**
Under 61	28	29	29					
61–70	28	29	30	30				
71–80	28	29	30	30	31			
81–90	29	29	30	30	31	32		
91–100	29	30	30	31	31	32		
101–110	29	30	30	31	31	32		
111–120	29	30	30	31	31	32		
121–130	29	30	30	31	32	33	33	
131–140	30	30	31	31	32	33	33	
141–150	30	30	31	31	32	33	33	
151–160	30	31	31	32	32	33	33	33
161–170		31	31	32	32	33	33	34
171–180				32	33	33	34	34
Over 180					33	33	34	34

3.4 **Writing Proportions** (continued)

3 **ACTIVITY:** Checking a Proportion

Work with a partner. The batting average of a baseball player is the number of "hits" divided by the number of "at bats."

$$\text{Batting Average} = \frac{\text{Hits } (H)}{\text{At Bats } (A)}$$

A player whose batting average is 0.250 is said to be "batting 250."

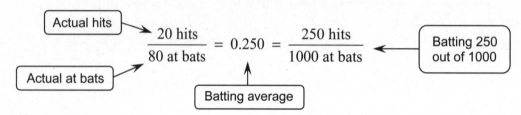

Actual hits

$$\frac{20 \text{ hits}}{80 \text{ at bats}} = 0.250 = \frac{250 \text{ hits}}{1000 \text{ at bats}}$$

Actual at bats

Batting average

Batting 250 out of 1000

Write a proportion to find how many hits *H* a player needs to achieve the given batting average. Then solve the proportion.

a. 50 times at bat
batting average is 0.200.

b. 84 times at bat
batting average is 0.250.

c. 80 times at bat
batting average is 0.350.

d. 1 time at bat
batting average is 1.000.

3.4 **Writing Proportions** (continued)

What Is Your Answer?

4. IN YOUR OWN WORDS How can you write a proportion that solves a problem in real life?

5. Two players have the same batting average.

	At Bats	Hits	Batting Average
Player 1	132	45	
Player 2	132	45	

Player 1 gets four hits in the next five at bats. Player 2 gets three hits in the next three at bats.

a. Who has the higher batting average?

b. Does this seem fair? Explain your reasoning.

Name _____ Date _____

Write a proportion to find how many points a student needs to score on the test to get the given score.

1. Test worth 50 points; test score of 84%

2. Test worth 75 points; test score of 96%

Use the table to write a proportion.

3.

	Trip 1	Trip 2
Miles	104	78
Gallons	4	g

4.

	Tree 1	Tree 2
Inches	15	x
Years	4	3

Solve the proportion.

5. $\dfrac{1}{3} = \dfrac{x}{12}$

6. $\dfrac{5}{9} = \dfrac{25}{y}$

7. $\dfrac{26}{z} = \dfrac{13}{22}$

8. $\dfrac{b}{30} = \dfrac{2.6}{1.5}$

9. A local Humane Society houses 300 animals. The ratio of cats to all animals is 7 : 15.

   a. Write a proportion that gives the number of cats c.

   b. How many cats are in the Humane Society?

10. Your school buys 30 graphing calculators for $1822.50. Write and solve a proportion that gives the cost c of buying 120 calculators.

3.5 Solving Proportions
For use with Activity 3.5

Essential Question How can you use ratio tables and cross products to solve proportions in science?

---

1 **ACTIVITY:** Solving a Proportion in Science

SCIENCE Scientists use *ratio tables* to determine the amount of a compound (like salt) that is dissolved in a solution. Work with a partner to show how scientists use cross products to determine the unknown quantity in a ratio.

a. **Sample:** Salt Water

Salt Water	1 L	3 L
Salt	250 g	x g

1 liter   3 liter

There are _____ grams of salt in the 3-liter solution.

b. **White Glue Solution**

Water	$\frac{1}{2}$ cup	1 cup
White Glue	$\frac{1}{2}$ cup	x cups

c. **Borax Solution**

Borax	1 tsp	2 tsp
Water	1 cup	x cups

3.5 **Solving Proportions** (continued)

d. **Slime** (see recipe)

Borax Solution	$\dfrac{1}{2}$ cup	1 cup
White Glue Solution	y cups	x cups

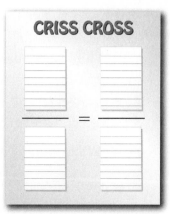

Recipe for SLIME

1. Add ½ cup of water and ½ cup white glue. Mix thoroughly. This is your white glue solution.

2. Add a couple drops of food coloring to the glue solution. Mix thoroughly.

3. Add 1 teaspoon of borax to 1 cup of water. Mix thoroughly. This is your borax solution (about 1 cup).

4. Pour the borax solution and the glue solution into a separate bowl.

5. Place the slime that forms in a plastic bag and squeeze the mixture repeatedly to mix it up.

2   ACTIVITY: The Game of Criss Cross

Preparation:

- Cut index cards to make 48 playing cards.

- Write each number on a card.
  1, 1, 1, 2, 2, 2, 3, 3, 3, 4, 4, 4, 5, 5, 5, 6, 6, 6, 7, 7, 7, 8, 8, 8, 9, 9, 9, 10, 10, 10, 12, 12, 12, 13, 13, 13, 14, 14, 14, 15, 15, 15, 16, 16, 16, 18, 20, 25

- Make a copy of the game board.

CRISS CROSS

To Play:

- Play with a partner.

- Deal 8 cards to each player.

- Begin by drawing a card from the remaining cards. Use four of your cards to try and form a proportion.

- Lay the four cards on the game board. If you form a proportion, say "Criss Cross" and you earn 4 points. Place the four cards in a discard pile. Now it is your partner's turn.

- If you cannot form a proportion, then it is your partner's turn.

- When the original pile of cards is empty, shuffle the cards in the discard pile and start again.

- The first player to reach 20 points wins.

3.5 **Solving Proportions** (continued)

What Is Your Answer?

3. **IN YOUR OWN WORDS** How can you use ratio tables and cross products to solve proportions in science? Give an example.

4. **PUZZLE** Use each number once to form three proportions.

1	2	10	4	12	20
15	5	16	6	8	3

Name _____ Date _____

Solve the proportion using multiplication.

1. $\dfrac{a}{40} = \dfrac{3}{10}$

2. $\dfrac{6}{11} = \dfrac{c}{77}$

3. $\dfrac{b}{65} = \dfrac{7}{13}$

Solve the proportion using the Cross Products Property.

4. $\dfrac{k}{6} = \dfrac{8}{16}$

5. $\dfrac{5.4}{7} = \dfrac{27}{h}$

6. $\dfrac{15}{n} = \dfrac{20}{8}$

Solve the proportion.

7. $\dfrac{5}{2} = \dfrac{4x}{8}$

8. $\dfrac{8}{11} = \dfrac{4}{y+2}$

9. $\dfrac{3}{z-1} = \dfrac{9}{15}$

10. A cell phone company charges $5 for 250 text messages. How much does the company charge for 300 text messages?

11. There are 84 players on a football team. The ratio of offensive players to defensive players is 4 to 3. How many offensive players are on the team?

3.6 Converting Measures Between Systems
For use with Activity 3.6

Essential Question How can you compare lengths between the customary and metric systems?

Work with a partner.

a. Match the measure of length with its historical beginning.

Length	*Historical Beginning*
Inch	The length of a human foot.
Foot	The width of a human thumb.
Yard	The distance a human can walk in 1000 paces (two steps).
Mile	The distance from a human nose to the end of an outstretched human arm.

b. Use a ruler to measure your thumb, arm, and foot. How do your measurements compare to your answers from part (a)? Are they close to the historical measures?

You already know how to convert measures within the customary and metric systems.

Equivalent Customary Lengths

> 1 ft = 12 in.   1 yd = 3 ft   1 mi = 5280 ft

Equivalent Metric Lengths

> 1 m = 1000 mm   1 m = 100 cm   1 km = 1000 m

You will learn how to convert between the two systems.

Converting Between Systems

1 in. ≈ 2.54 cm

1 mi ≈ 1.6 km

2.54 cm

1 in.

3.6   **Converting Measures Between Systems** (continued)

2 **ACTIVITY:** Comparing Measures

Work with a partner. Answer each question. Explain your answer. Use a diagram in your explanation.

	Metric	*Customary*
a. Car Speed: Which is faster?	80 km/h	60 mi/h
b. Trip Distance: Which is farther?	200 km	200 mi
c. Human Height: Who is taller?	180 cm	5 ft 8 in.
d. Wrench Width: Which is wider?	8 mm	5/16 in.
e. Swimming Pool Depth: Which is deeper?	1.4 m	4 ft
f. Mountain Elevation: Which is higher?	2000 m	7000 ft
g. Room Width: Which is wider?	3.5 m	12 ft

3.6 **Converting Measures Between Systems** (continued)

What Is Your Answer?

3. **IN YOUR OWN WORDS** How can you compare lengths between the customary and metric systems? Give examples with your description.

4. **HISTORY** The meter and the metric system originated in France. In 1791, the French Academy of Sciences was instructed to create a new system of measurement. This new system would be based on powers of 10.

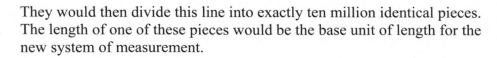

North Pole

Meter = 1 ten-millionth of this distance

Equator

The fundamental units of this system would be based on natural values that were unchanging. The French Academy of Sciences decided to find the length of an imaginary arc that began at the North Pole and ended at the equator.

They would then divide this line into exactly ten million identical pieces. The length of one of these pieces would be the base unit of length for the new system of measurement.

a. Find the distance around Earth in meters.

b. Find the distance around Earth in kilometers.

5. Find the distance around Earth in miles.

3.6 Practice
For use after Lesson 3.6

Complete the statement using a ratio. Round to the nearest hundredth, if necessary.

1. 10 mi ≈ _____ km

2. 15 kg ≈ _____ lb

3. 6 qt ≈ _____ L

Complete the statement using < or >.

4. 11 in. _____ 22 cm

5. 12 kg _____ 500 oz

6. 8 gal _____ 25 L

7. 10 m _____ 30 ft

Complete the statement. Round to the nearest hundredth, if necessary.

8. 60 mi/h ≈ _____ km/h

9. 6 ft/sec ≈ _____ cm/sec

10. 52 gal/min ≈ _____ L/min

11. 5 kg/day ≈ _____ oz/day

12. One lap around a high school track is 400 meters. How many laps do you run around the track if you run 2 miles?

13. A doctor prescribes 200 milligrams of medicine for a patient. How many ounces of medicine is the patient taking?

14. The lightest weight class for young men competing in freestyle wrestling is from 29 kilograms to 32 kilograms. What is the range of the weight class in pounds?

3.7 Direct Variation
For use with Activity 3.7

Essential Question How can you use a graph to show the relationship between two variables that vary directly? How can you use an equation?

1 ACTIVITY: Math in Literature

Gulliver's Travels was written by Jonathan Swift and published in 1725. Gulliver was shipwrecked on an island in Lilliput, where the people were only 6 inches tall. When the Lilliputians decided to make a shirt for Gulliver, a Lilliputian tailor stated that he could determine Gulliver's measurements by simply measuring the distance around Gulliver's thumb. He said "Twice around the thumb equals once around the wrist. Twice around the wrist is once around the neck. Twice around the neck is once around the waist."

Work with a partner. Use the tailor's statement to complete the table.

Thumb, t	Wrist, w	Neck, n	Waist, x
0 in.	0 in.		
1 in.	2 in.		
2 in.	4 in.		
3 in.	6 in.		
4 in.	8 in.		
5 in.	10 in.		

3.7 Direct Variation (continued)

2 **EXAMPLE:** Drawing a Graph

Use the information from Activity 1 to draw a graph of the relationship between the distance around the thumb *t* and the distance around the wrist *w*.

Use the table to write ordered pairs. Then plot the ordered pairs.

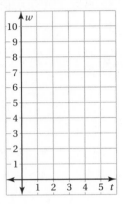

What do you notice about the graph?

This type of relationship is called **direct variation**. You can write an equation to describe the relationship between *t* and *w*.

$w = 2t$ Wrist is twice thumb.

3 **ACTIVITY:** Drawing a Graph

Work with a partner. Use the information from Activity 1 to draw a graph of the relationship. Write an equation that describes the relationship between the two variables.

a. Thumb *t* and neck *n*

$$\left(n = \boxed{} \ t \right)$$

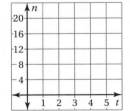

b. Wrist *w* and waist *x*

$$\left(x = \boxed{} \ w \right)$$

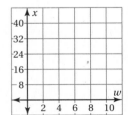

3.7 **Direct Variation** (continued)

c. Wrist w and thumb t

$$\left(t = \boxed{} \; w \right)$$

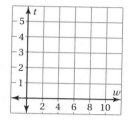

d. Waist x and wrist w

$$\left(w = \boxed{} \; x \right)$$

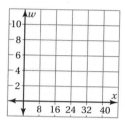

What Is Your Answer?

4. IN YOUR OWN WORDS How can you use a graph to show the relationship between two variables that vary directly? How can you use an equation?

5. Give a real-life example of two variables that vary directly.

6. Work with a partner. Use string to find the distance around your thumb, wrist, and neck. Do your measurements agree with those of the tailor in *Gulliver's Travels*? Explain your reasoning.

3.7 Practice
For use after Lesson 3.7

Tell whether x and y show direct variation. Explain your reasoning.

1.

x	1	2	3	4
y	3	6	9	12

2.

x	−1	0	1	2
y	1	3	7	13

3.

x	0	2	4	6
y	8	5	2	−1

4. $y + 2 = x$

5. $3y = x$

6. $\dfrac{y}{x} = 4$

The variables x and y vary directly. Use the values to write an equation that relates x and y.

7. $y = 8;\ x = 2$

8. $y = 14,\ x = 16$

9. $y = 25,\ x = 35$

10. The table shows the cups c of dog food needed to feed a dog that weighs p pounds. Tell whether p and c show direct variation.

Pounds, p	10	20	40	70
Food, c	$\dfrac{3}{4}$	$1\dfrac{1}{4}$	2	$2\dfrac{3}{4}$

11. Write a direct variation equation that relates x tires to y cars.

12. Tell whether h and m show direct variation. If so, write an equation of direct variation.

Hours, h	1	2	4	5
Miles, m	60.5	121	242	302.5

Name_____ Date_____

3.8 Inverse Variation
For use with Activity 3.8

Essential Question How can you recognize when two variables are inversely proportional?

1 ACTIVITY: Comparing the Height and the Base

Work with a partner.

   a. There are nine ways to arrange 36 square blocks to form a rectangle. Here are two ways. Draw the other seven ways.

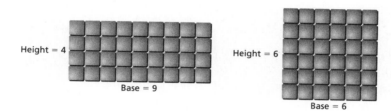

   b. Order the nine ways according to height. Record your results in the table.

Height, *h*	Base, *b*	Area, *A*

3.8 **Inverse Variation** (continued)

c. Look at the first and second columns of the table. Complete each sentence.

- When the height increases, the base _____.
- When the height decreases, the base _____.

In Activity 1, the relationship between the height and base is an example of **inverse variation**. You can describe the relationship with an equation.

$$h = \frac{36}{b}$$ h and b are inversely proportional.

2 **ACTIVITY:** Comparing Direct and Inverse Variation

Work with a partner. Discuss each description. Tell whether the two variables are examples of *direct variation* or *inverse variation*. Use a table to explain your reasoning. Write an equation that relates the variables.

a. You bring 200 cookies to a party. Let n represent the number of people at the party and c represent the number of cookies each person receives.

b. You work at a restaurant for 20 hours. Let r represent your hourly pay rate and p represent the total amount you earn.

c. You are going on a 240-mile trip. Let t represent the number of hours driving and s represent the speed of the car.

3.8   **Inverse Variation** (continued)

What Is Your Answer?

3. **IN YOUR OWN WORDS** How can you recognize when two variables are inversely proportional? Explain how a table can help you recognize inverse variation.

4. **SCIENCE** The *wing beat frequency* of a bird is the number of times per second the bird flaps its wings.

Hummingbird

Mallard Duck

Canada Goose

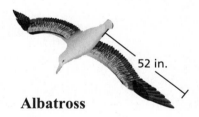

Albatross

Which of the following seems true? Explain your reasoning.

*   Wing length and wing beat frequency are directly proportional.

*   Wing length and wing beat frequency are inversely proportional.

*   Wing length and wing beat frequency are unrelated.

5. **SCIENCE** Think of an example in science where two variables are inversely proportional.

3.8 Practice
For use after Lesson 3.8

Tell whether *x* and *y* show *direct variation*, *inverse variation*, or *neither*.
Explain your reasoning.

1. $2y = 3x + 1$ **2.** $\dfrac{y}{5} = \dfrac{6}{x}$ **3.** $\dfrac{y}{x} = 4$ **4.** $xy = 2$

The variables *x* and *y* vary inversely. Write an equation relating *x* and *y*.

5.
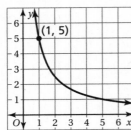

6.
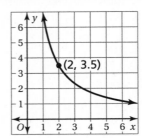

7. You have 1.5 pounds of spaghetti. When you make dinner for four people, each person is served 6 ounces of spaghetti.

   a. Complete the table. Does the serving size *s* vary inversely with the number of people *p*? If so, write an equation relating *s* and *p*.

People, *p*	Serving Size, *s*
2	
4	6
6	

   b. How much spaghetti will each person receive if you are serving five people?

Name_____ Date_____

What percent of the model is shaded?

1.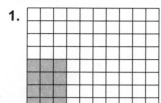

2.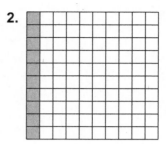

3.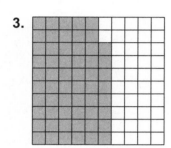

4.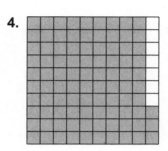

Write the fraction as a decimal or the decimal as a fraction.

5. $\dfrac{5}{8}$

6. $\dfrac{21}{40}$

7. 0.26

8. 0.79

9. In your class, 0.65 of the students are wearing sneakers. What fraction of students are wearing sneakers?

Name_____ Date _____

Write the fraction as a percent or the percent as a fraction.

10. $\dfrac{13}{20}$

11. $\dfrac{47}{50}$

12. 52%

13. 31%

Write the decimal as a percent or the percent as a decimal.

14. 0.06

15. 0.84

16. 22%

17. 191%

Complete the table.

	Percent	Decimal	Fraction
18.	45%		
19.		0.73	
20.			$\dfrac{3}{10}$

4.1 The Percent Equation
For use with Activity 4.1

Essential Question How can you use models to estimate percent questions?

---

1 ACTIVITY: Estimating a Percent

Work with a partner. Estimate the locations of 50%, 75%, 40%, 6%, and 65% on the model. 50% is done for you.

```
0%                    50%                 100%
[_____|_____]
```

---

2 ACTIVITY: Estimating a Part of a Number

The statement "25% of 12 is 3" has three numbers. In real-life problems, any one of these can be unknown.

$$\frac{3}{12} = 0.25 = 25\%$$

Part → 3

Whole → 12

Percent ←

Which number is missing?	Question	Type of Question
_____	What is 25% of 12?	Find a part of a number.
_____	3 is what percent of 12?	Find a percent.
_____	3 is 25% of what?	Find a percent.

Work with a partner. Estimate the answer to each question using a model.

a. What number is 50% of 30?

```
0%                                      100%
[_____]
0                                        30
```

Big Ideas Math Red **89**
Record and Practice Journal

4.1 **The Percent Equation** (continued)

b. What number is 75% of 30?

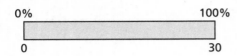

c. What number is 40% of 30?

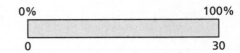

d. What number is 6% of 30?

0%   100%

0   30

e. What number is 65% of 30?

0%   100%

0   30

---

3 **ACTIVITY:** Estimating a Percent

Work with a partner. Estimate the answer to the question using a model.

a. 15 is what percent of 75?

b. 5 is what percent of 20?

c. 18 is what percent of 40?

d. 50 is what percent of 80?

0%   100%

0   80

e. 75 is what percent of 50?

0%   100%

0   50

4.1 The Percent Equation **(continued)**

4 **ACTIVITY:** Estimating a Percent

Work with a partner. Estimate the answer to the question using a model.

a. 24 is $33\frac{1}{3}\%$ of what number?

0%   100%

b. 13 is 25% of what number?

0%   100%

c. 110 is 20% of what number?

0%   100%

d. 75 is 75% of what number?

0%   100%

e. 81 is 45% of what number?

0%   100%

What Is Your Answer?

5. IN YOUR OWN WORDS How can you use models to estimate percent questions? Give examples to support your answer.

Name _____ Date _____

Write and solve an equation to answer the question.

1. 40% of 60 is what number?

2. 17 is what percent of 50?

3. 38% of what number is 57?

4. 44% of 25 is what number?

5. 52 is what percent of 50?

6. 150% of what number is 18?

7. You put 60% of your paycheck into your savings account. Your paycheck is $235. How much money do you put in your savings account?

8. You made lemonade and iced tea for a school fair. You made 15 gallons of lemonade and 60% is gone. About 52% of the iced tea is gone. The ratio of gallons of lemonade to gallons of iced tea was 3 : 2.

   a. How many gallons of lemonade are left?

   b. How many gallons of iced tea did you make?

   c. About how many gallons of iced tea are left?

4.2 Percents of Increase and Decrease
For use with Activity 4.2

Essential Question What is a percent of decrease? What is a percent of increase?

1 ACTIVITY: Percent of Decrease

Each year in the Columbia River Basin, adult salmon swim up river to streams to lay eggs and hatch their young.

To go up river, the adult salmon use fish ladders. But, to go down the river, the young salmon must pass through several dams.

There are electric turbines at each of the eight dams on the main stem of the Columbia and Snake Rivers. About 88% of the young salmon pass through these turbines unharmed.

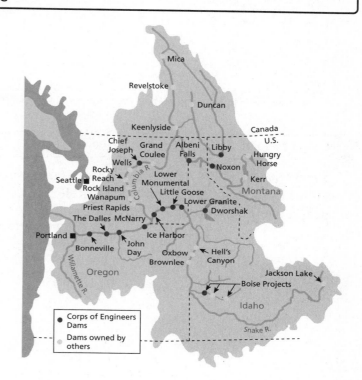

Complete the table to show the number of young salmon that make it through the dams.

Dam	0	1	2	3	4	5	6	7	8
Salmon	1000								

4.2 Percents of Increase and Decrease (continued)

Use the table you made on the previous page to complete the bar graph.

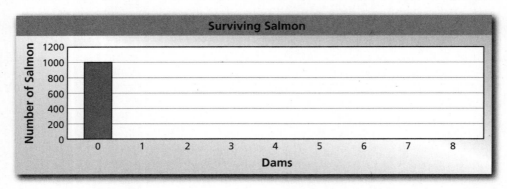

Surviving Salmon

2 ACTIVITY: Percent of Increase

From 2000 to 2006, the population of Florida increased about 2% each year. Complete the table and the bar graph using this pattern. Predict the population for 2015.

For 2007:

$$2\% \text{ of } 18{,}000{,}000 = 0.02 \bullet 18{,}000{,}000$$
$$= 360{,}000$$

$$18{,}000{,}000 + 360{,}000 = 18{,}360{,}000$$

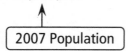

2006 Population   Increase   2007 Population

2006 Population 18,000,000

Year	Population
2006	18,000,000
2007	18,360,000
2008	
2009	
2010	
2011	
2012	
2013	
2014	
2015	

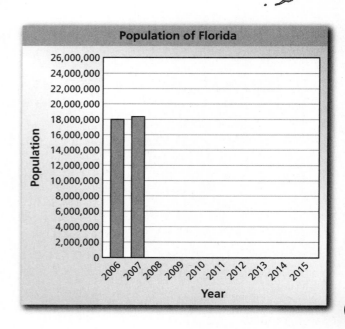

Population of Florida

4.2 Percents of Increase and Decrease (continued)

What Is Your Answer?

3. In Activity 1, by what percent does the number of young salmon decrease with each dam?

4. Describe real-life examples of a percent of decrease and a percent of increase.

5. IN YOUR OWN WORDS What is a percent of decrease? What is a percent of increase?

Name _____ Date _____

4.2 Practice

For use after Lesson 4.2

Identify the percent of change as an *increase* or *decrease*. Then find the percent of change. Round to the nearest tenth of a percent, if necessary.

1. 25 points to 50 points

2. 125 invitations to 75 invitations

3. 32 pages to 28 pages

4. 7 players to 10 players

Find the new amount.

5. 120 books increased by 55%

6. 80 members decreased by 65%

7. One week, 72 people got a speeding ticket. The next week, only 36 people got a speeding ticket. What is the percent of change in speeding tickets?

8. The number of athletes participating in the Paralympics rose from 130 athletes in 1952 to 3806 athletes in 2004. What is the percent of change? Round your answer to the nearest tenth of a percent.

Name_____ Date_____

4.3 **Discounts and Markups**
For use with Activity 4.3

Essential Question How can you find discounts and markups efficiently?

---

1 **ACTIVITY:** Comparing Discounts

Work with a partner. The same pair of sneakers is on sale at three stores. Which one is the best buy?

a. Regular Price: $45   b. Regular Price: $49   c. Regular Price: $39

a.
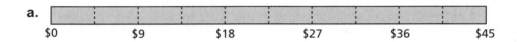

b.
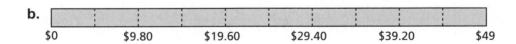

c.
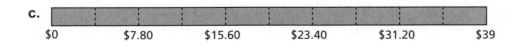

4.3 **Discounts and Markups** (continued)

2 **ACTIVITY:** Finding the Original Price

Work with a partner. You buy a shirt that is on sale for 30% off. You pay $22.40. Your friend wants to know the original price of the shirt. How can your friend find the original price?

$0 $22.40   Original Price

3 **ACTIVITY:** Calculating Markup

You own a small jewelry store. You increase the price of jewelry by 125%.

Work with a partner. Use a model to estimate the selling price of the jewelry. Then use a calculator to find the selling price.

a. Your cost is $250.

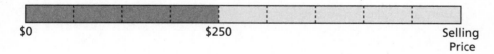

$0 $250   Selling Price

4.3 Discounts and Markups (continued)

b. Your cost is $50.

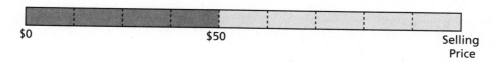

$0 $50   Selling
                                                       Price

c. Your cost is $20.

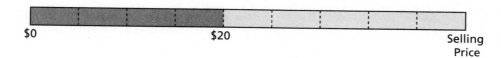

$0 $20   Selling
                                                       Price

What Is Your Answer?

4. **IN YOUR OWN WORDS** How can you find discounts and markups
   efficiently? Give examples of each.

Practice
For use after Lesson 4.3

Complete the table.

	Original Price	Percent of Discount	Sale Price
1.	$20	20%	
2.	$95	35%	
3.		75%	$55.50
4.		40%	$78

Find the cost to store, percent of markup, or selling price.

5. Cost to store: $20
Markup: 15%
Selling price: ?

6. Cost to store: ?
Markup: 80%
Selling Price: $100.80

7. Cost to store: $110
Markup: ?
Selling price: $264

8. A store buys an item for $10. To earn a profit of $25, what percent does the store need to markup the item?

9. Your dinner at a restaurant costs $13.65 after you use a coupon for a 25% discount. You leave a tip for $3.00.

a. How much was your dinner before the discount?

b. You tip your server based on the price before the discount. What percent tip did you leave? Round your answer to the nearest tenth of a percent.

Name_____ Date _____

Essential Question How can you find the amount of simple interest earned on a savings account? How can you find the amount of interest owed on a loan?

Simple interest is money earned on a savings account or an investment. It can also be money you pay for borrowing money.

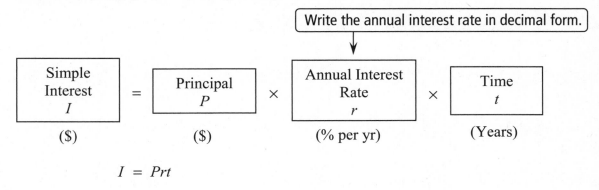

Write the annual interest rate in decimal form.

Simple Interest I	=	Principal P	×	Annual Interest Rate r	×	Time t
($)		($)		(% per yr)		(Years)

$$I = Prt$$

---

1 **ACTIVITY:** Finding Simple Interest

Work with a partner. You put $100 in a savings account. The account earns 6% simple interest per year. (a) Find the interest earned and the balance at the end of 6 months. (b) Complete the table. Then make a bar graph that shows how the balance grows in 6 months.

a. $I = Prt$

b.

Time	Interest	Balance
0 month		
1 month		
2 months		
3 months		
4 months		
5 months		
6 months		

4.4 **Simple Interest** (continued)

2 **ACTIVITY:** Financial Literacy

Work with a partner. Use the following information to write a report about credit cards. In the report, describe how a credit card works. Include examples that show the amount of interest paid each month on a credit card.

U.S. Credit Card Data

- A typical family in the United States owes about $5000 in credit card debt.

- A typical credit card interest rate is 18% to 20% per year. This is called the annual percentage rate.

3 **ACTIVITY:** The National Debt

Work with a partner. In 2010, the United States owed about $10 trillion in debt. The interest rate on the national debt is about 3% per year.

a. Write $10 trillion in decimal form. How many zeros does this number have?

4.4 **Simple Interest** (continued)

b. How much interest does the United States pay each year on its national debt?

c. How much interest does the United States pay each day on its national debt?

d. The United States has a population of about 300 million people. Estimate the amount of interest that each person pays per year toward interest on the national debt.

What Is Your Answer?

4. **IN YOUR OWN WORDS** How can you find the amount of simple interest earned on a savings account? How can you find the amount of interest owed on a loan? Give examples with your answer.

4.4 **Practice**
For use after Lesson 4.4

An account earns simple interest. (a) Find the interest earned. (b) Find the balance of the account.

   1. $400 at 7% for 3 years

   2. $1200 at 5.6% for 4 years

Find the annual simple interest rate.

   3. $I = \$18$, $P = \$200$, $t = 18$ months

   4. $I = \$310$, $P = \$1000$, $t = 5$ years

Find the amount of time.

   5. $I = \$60$, $P = \$750$, $r = 4\%$

   6. $I = \$825$, $P = \$2500$, $r = 5.5\%$

   7. You put $500 in a savings account. The account earns $15.75 simple interest in 6 months. What is the annual interest rate?

   8. You put $1000 in an account. The simple interest rate is 4.5%. After a year, you put in another $550. What is your total interest after 2 years from the time you opened the account?

Chapter 5 Fair Game Review

Find the perimeter or circumference.

1.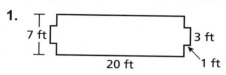
7 ft 3 ft 1 ft 20 ft

2.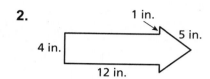
1 in. 5 in. 4 in. 12 in.

3.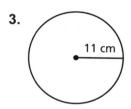
11 cm

4.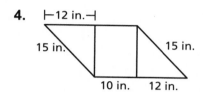
12 in. 15 in. 15 in. 10 in. 12 in.

5.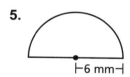
6 mm

6.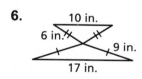
10 in. 6 in. 9 in. 17 in.

7. A restaurant sets up tables for a party in a U-shape. What is the perimeter of the tables?

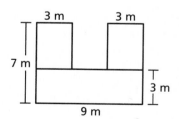
3 m 3 m 7 m 3 m 9 m

Name _____ Date _____

Solve the proportion.

8. $\dfrac{x}{20} = \dfrac{4}{5}$

9. $\dfrac{6}{x} = \dfrac{9}{12}$

10. $\dfrac{4}{9} = \dfrac{5}{x}$

11. $\dfrac{2x}{21} = \dfrac{2}{7}$

12. $\dfrac{18}{5x} = \dfrac{3}{5}$

13. $\dfrac{9}{10} = \dfrac{108}{10x}$

14. A flower shop sells a dozen roses for $25. How much does it cost to buy 18 roses?

5.1 Identifying Similar Figures
For use with Activity 5.1

Essential Question How can you use proportions to help make decisions in art, design, and magazine layouts?

Original Photograph

In a computer art program, when you click and drag on a side of a photograph, you distort it.

But when you click and drag on a corner of the photograph, it remains proportional to the original.

Distorted

Distorted

Proportional

1 ACTIVITY: Reducing Photographs

Work with a partner. You are trying to reduce the photograph to the indicated size for a nature magazine. Can you reduce the photograph to the indicated size without distorting or cropping? Explain your reasoning.

a.

5 in.

6 in.

4 in.

5 in.

b.

5 in.

5 in.

4 in.

4 in.

c.

6 in.

8 in.

3 in.

4 in.

5.1   **Identifying Similar Figures** (continued)

2   **ACTIVITY:** Proportional Designs

Work with a partner.

   a. Tell whether the new designs are proportional to the original design. Explain your reasoning.

Original	Design 1	Design 2

   b. Draw two designs that are proportional to the given design. Make one bigger and one smaller. Label the sides of the designs with their lengths.

      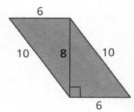

5.1 Identifying Similar Figures (continued)

What Is Your Answer?

3. **IN YOUR OWN WORDS** How can you use proportions to help make decisions in art, design, and magazine layouts? Give two examples.

4. **a.** Use a computer art program to draw two rectangles that are proportional to each other.

   b. Print the two rectangles on the same piece of paper.

   c. Use a centimeter ruler to measure the length and width of each rectangle. Record your measurements here.

"I love this statue. It seems similar to a big statue I saw in New York."

   d. Find the following ratios. What can you conclude?

   $$\frac{\text{Length of Larger}}{\text{Length of Smaller}} \qquad \frac{\text{Width of Larger}}{\text{Width of Smaller}}$$

Name _____ Date _____

Name the corresponding angles and the corresponding sides of the similar figures.

1.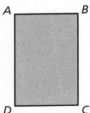

2.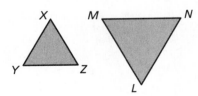

Tell whether the two figures are similar. Explain your reasoning.

3.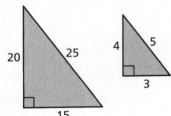

4.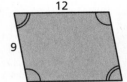

5. In your classroom, a dry erase board is 8 feet long and 4 feet wide. Your teacher makes individual dry erase boards for you to use at your desk that are 11.5 inches long and 9.5 inches wide. Are the boards similar?

6. You have a 4 x 6 photo of you and your friend.

   a. You order a 5 x 7 print of the photo. Is the new photo similar to the original?

   b. You enlarge the original photo to three times its size on your computer. Is the new photo similar to the original?

5.2 ## Perimeters and Areas of Similar Figures
For use with Activity 5.2

Essential Question How do changes in dimensions of similar geometric figures affect the perimeters and areas of the figures?

1 **ACTIVITY:** Comparing Perimeters and Areas

Work with a partner. Use pattern blocks to make a figure whose dimensions are 2, 3, and 4 times greater than those of the original figure. Find the perimeter P and area A of each larger figure.

a. Square

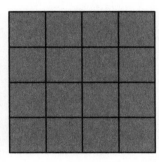

$P = 4$ $P = $ _____ $P = $ _____ $P = $ _____

$A = 1$ $A = $ _____ $A = $ _____ $A = $ _____

b. Triangle

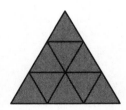
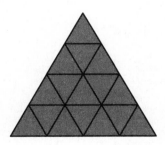

$P = 3$ $P = $ _____ $P = $ _____ $P = $ _____

$A = B$ $A = $ _____ $A = $ _____ $A = $ _____

5.2 Perimeters and Areas of Similar Figures (continued)

c. Rectangle

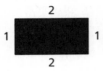

$$P = 6$$
$$A = 2$$

d. Parallelogram

$$P = 4$$
$$A = C$$

---

2 **ACTIVITY:** Finding Patterns for Perimeters

Work with a partner. Complete the table for the perimeters of the figures in Activity 1. Describe the pattern.

Figure	Original Side Lengths	Double Side Lengths	Triple Side Lengths	Quadruple Side Lengths
■	$P = 4$			
▲	$P = 3$			
▬	$P = 6$			
▰	$P = 4$			

5.2 **Perimeters and Areas of Similar Figures** (continued)

3 **ACTIVITY:** Finding Patterns for Areas

Work with a partner. Complete the table for the areas of the figures in
Activity 1. Describe the pattern.

Figure	Original Side Lengths	Double Side Lengths	Triple Side Lengths	Quadruple Side Lengths
	$A = 1$			
	$A = B$			
	$A = 2$			
	$A = C$			

What Is Your Answer?

4. **IN YOUR OWN WORDS** How do changes in dimensions of similar
   geometric figures affect the perimeters and areas of the figures?

5.2 **Practice**
For use after Lesson 5.2

The two figures are similar. Find the ratios (shaded to nonshaded) of the perimeters and of the areas.

1.

8   3

2.

6   10

3.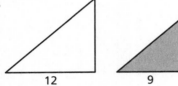

12   9

4.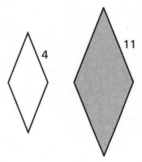

4   11

5. You buy two picture frames that are similar. The ratio of the corresponding side lengths is 4 : 5. What is the ratio of the areas?

6. Rectangle A is similar to Rectangle B. What is the ratio of the perimeter of Rectangle A to the perimeter of Rectangle B?

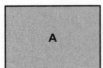

A   B

Area = 81 cm^2 Area = 16 cm^2

5.3 Finding Unknown Measures in Similar Figures
For use with Activity 5.3

Essential Question What information do you need to know to find the dimensions of a figure that is similar to another figure?

1 ACTIVITY: Drawing and Labeling Similar Figures

Work with a partner. You are given the rectangle. Find another rectangle that is similar and has one side from $(-1, -6)$ to $(5, -6)$. Label the vertices.

a.

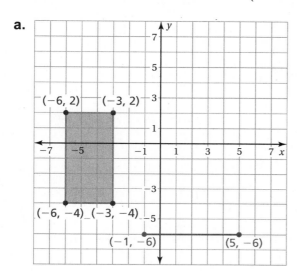

You can see that the two rectangles are similar by showing that ratios of corresponding sides are equal. Complete the steps below. Are the two rectangles above similar?

$$\frac{\text{Shaded Length}}{\text{Unshaded Length}} \overset{?}{=} \frac{\text{Shaded Width}}{\text{Unshaded Length}}$$

$$\frac{\text{change in } y}{\text{change in } y} \overset{?}{=} \frac{\text{change in } x}{\text{change in } x}$$

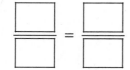

5.3 **Finding Unknown Measures in Similar Figures** (continued)

b. There are three other rectangles that are similar to the shaded rectangle and have the given side.

- Draw each one. Label the vertices of each.

- Show that each is similar to the original shaded rectangle.

2 **ACTIVITY:** Reading a Map

Work with a partner.

a. The rectangles are similar. Find the length of the larger rectangle. Explain your reasoning.

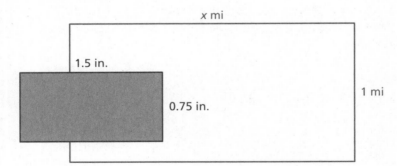

5.3 Finding Unknown Measures in Similar Figures (continued)

b. The distance marked by the vertical line on the map is 1 mile. Find the distance marked by the horizontal line. Explain your reasoning.

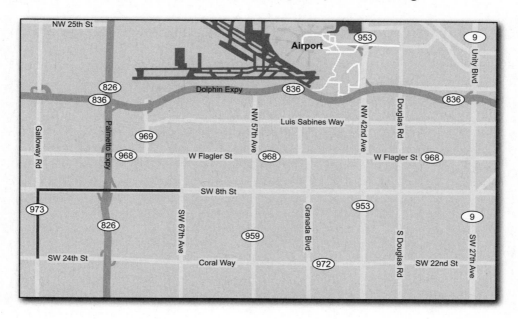

What Is Your Answer?

3. IN YOUR OWN WORDS What information do you need to know to find the dimensions of a figure that is similar to another figure? Give some examples using two rectangles.

4. When you know the length and width of one rectangle and the length of a similar rectangle, can you always find the missing width? Why or why not?

5.3 Practice
For use after Lesson 5.3

The polygons are similar. Find the value of x.

1.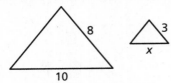

2.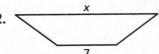

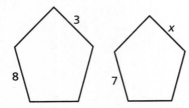

3. 4. The ratio of the perimeters is 2 : 5.

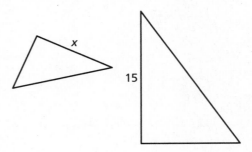

5. A tree casts a shadow that is 50 feet long. A 4-foot person casts a shadow that is 10 feet long. How tall is the tree?

6. A cookie sheet is 12 inches wide and has a perimeter of 52 inches. You buy a similar cookie sheet that is 15 inches wide. What is its perimeter?

Name_____ Date _____

5.4 Scale Drawings
For use with Activity 5.4

Essential Question How can you use a scale drawing to estimate the cost of painting a room?

1 ACTIVITY: Making Scale Drawings

Work with a partner. You have decided that your classroom needs to be painted. Start by making a scale drawing of each of the four walls.

- Measure each of the walls.

- Measure the locations and dimensions of parts that will *not* be painted.

- Decide on a scale for your drawings.

- Make a scale drawing of each of the walls.

Sample: Wall #1

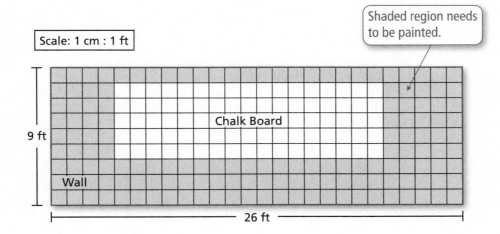

Scale: 1 cm : 1 ft

Shaded region needs to be painted.

Chalk Board

9 ft

Wall

26 ft

- For each wall, find the area of the part that needs to be painted.

	Dimensions	*Area*
Dimensions of the wall	9 ft by 26 ft	$9 \times 26 = 234$ sq ft
Dimensions of the part that will *not* be painted	5 ft by 17 ft	$5 \times 17 = 85$ sq ft
Area of painted part		$234 - 85 = 149$ sq ft

5.4 **Scale Drawings** (continued)

2 **ACTIVITY:** Using Scale Drawings

Work with a partner.

You are using a paint that covers 200 square feet per gallon. Each wall will need two coats of paint.

| Interior latex paint | $40 per gallon |
| Roller, pan, and brush set | $12 |

a. Find the total area of the walls in your classroom that need to be painted.

b. Find the amount of paint you need to buy.

c. Estimate the total cost of painting your classroom.

5.4 **Scale Drawings** (continued)

What Is Your Answer?

3. **IN YOUR OWN WORDS** How can you use a scale drawing to estimate the cost of painting a room?

4. Use a scale drawing to estimate the cost of painting another room, such as your bedroom or another room in your house.

5. Look at some maps in your school library or on the Internet. Make a list of the different scales used on the maps.

"I don't get it. According to this map, we only have to drive $8\frac{1}{2}$ inches."

6. When you view a map on the Internet, how does the scale change when you zoom out? How does the scale change when you zoom in?

5.4 Practice
For use after Lesson 5.4

Find the missing dimension. Use the scale factor 1 : 8.

Item	Model	Actual
1. Statue	Height: 168 in.	Height: _____ ft
2. Painting	Width: _____ cm	Width: 200 m
3. Alligator	Height: _____ in.	Height: 6.4 ft
4. Train	Length: 36.5 in.	Length: _____ ft

5. The diameter of the moon is 2160 miles. A model has a scale of 1 in. : 150 mi. What is the diameter of the model?

6. A map has a scale of 1 in. : 4 mi.

   a. You measure 3 inches between your house and the movie theater. How many miles is it from your house to the movie theater?

   b. It is 17 miles to the mall. How many inches is that on the map?

Translations
For use with Activity 5.5

Essential Question   How can you use translations to make
a tessellation?

When you slide a tile it is called a **translation**. When tiles can be used
to cover a floor with no empty spaces, the collection of tiles is called
a *tessellation*.

1   ACTIVITY: Describing Tessellations

**Work with a partner. Can you make the pattern by using a translation of single
tiles that are all of the same shape and design? If so, outline the single tile.**

   a. Sample:

Tile Pattern	Single Tiles

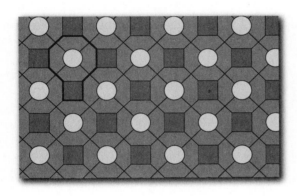   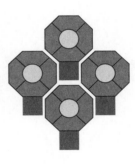

b.

c.

5.5 Translations (continued)

d.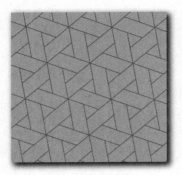

e.

2 ACTIVITY: Tessellations and Basic Shapes

Work with a partner.

a. Which pattern blocks can you use to make a tessellation?

b. For each pattern block you listed in part (a), draw the tessellation.

c. Can you make the tessellation using only translations, or do you have to rotate or flip the pattern blocks?

5.5 **Translations** (continued)

3 **ACTIVITY:** Designing Tessellations

Work with a partner. Design your own tessellation. Use one of the basic shapes from Activity 2.

Sample:

Start with
a square.

Cut a design out
of one side.

Tape it to the other side
to make your pattern.

- **Use your pattern and translations to make your tessellation.**
- **Color the tessellation.**

What Is Your Answer?

4. **IN YOUR OWN WORDS** How can you use translations to make a tessellation? Give an example.

5. Draw any parallelogram. Does it tessellate? Is it true that any parallelogram can be translated to make a tessellation? Explain why.

5.5 **Practice**
For use after Lesson 5.5

Tell whether the shaded figure is a translation of the nonshaded figure.

1.

2.

3.

4. Translate the figure 4 units left and 1 unit down. What are the coordinates of the image?

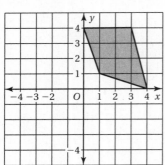

5. Translate the triangle 5 units right and 4 units up. What are the coordinates of the image?

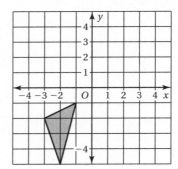

6. A rectangle is translated 3 units left and 4 units down. Then the image is translated 6 units right and 1 unit up. Write a translation of the original rectangle to the ending position.

7. Describe the translation from the shaded figure to the nonshaded figure.

5.6 Reflections
For use with Activity 5.6

Essential Question How can you use reflections to classify a frieze pattern?

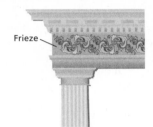

Frieze →

A *frieze* is a horizontal band that runs at the top of a building. A frieze is often decorated with a design that repeats.

- All frieze patterns are translations of themselves.
- Some frieze patterns are reflections of themselves.

---

1 EXAMPLE: Frieze Patterns

Is the frieze pattern a reflection of itself when folded horizontally? vertically?*

- Fold (reflect) on the horizontal axis. The pattern coincides.

- Fold (reflect) on the vertical axis. The pattern coincides.

The frieze pattern is a reflection of itself when it is folded horizontally *and* vertically.

---

2 ACTIVITY: Frieze Patterns and Reflections

Work with a partner. Is the frieze pattern a reflection of itself when folded *horizontally*, *vertically*, or *neither*?

a.

*Cut-outs are available in the back of the Record and Practice Journal.

5.6 **Reflections** (continued)

b.

c.

d.

e.

f.

5.6 **Reflections** (continued)

What Is Your Answer?

3. Draw a frieze pattern that is a reflection of itself when folded horizontally.

4. Draw a frieze pattern that is a reflection of itself when folded vertically.

5. Draw a frieze pattern that is not a reflection of itself when folded horizontally or vertically.

6. IN YOUR OWN WORDS How can you use reflections to classify a frieze pattern?

5.6 Practice
For use after Lesson 5.6

Tell whether the shaded figure is a reflection of the nonshaded figure.

1.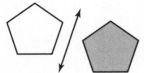

2.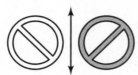

3.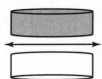

Find the coordinates of the figure after reflecting in the *x*-axis.

4. $A(1, 2)$, $B(3, 3)$, $C(0, 4)$

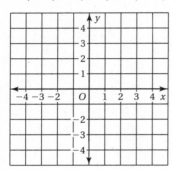

5. $W(4, 2)$, $X(3, 4)$, $Y(1, 3)$, $Z(3, 1)$

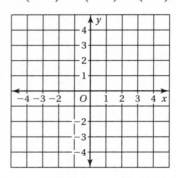

Find the coordinates of the figure after reflecting in the *y*-axis.

6. $J(3, 4)$, $K(4, 0)$, $L(2, 3)$

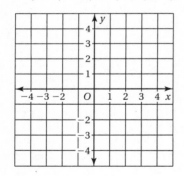

7. $M(2, 2)$, $N(2, 3)$, $P(3, 3)$, $Q(4, 1)$

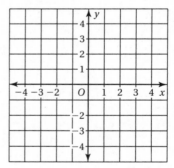

8. In a pinball game, if you perfectly reflect the ball off of the wall, will the ball hit the bonus target?

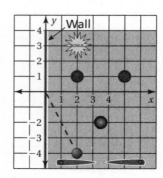

5.7 Rotations
For use with Activity 5.7

Essential Question What are the three basic ways to move an object in a plane?

1 ACTIVITY: Three Basic Ways to Move Things

There are three basic ways to move objects on a flat surface.

1. Translate the object. **2.** Reflect the object. **3.** Rotate the object.

  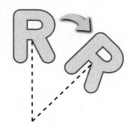

Work with a partner.

- Cut out a paper triangle that is the same size as the shaded triangle shown.*

- Decide how you can move the shaded triangle to make each nonshaded triangle.

- Is each move a *translation*, a *reflection*, or a *rotation*?

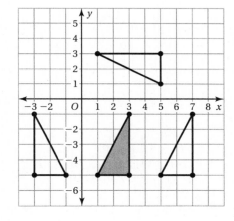

- Draw four other nonshaded triangles in a coordinate plane. Describe how you can move the shaded triangle to make each nonshaded triangle.

*Cut-outs are available in the back of the Record and Practice Journal.

5.7 **Rotations** (continued)

2 **ACTIVITY:** Tessellating a Plane

Work with a partner.

 a. Describe how the figure labeled 1 in each diagram can be moved to make
   the other figures.

Triangles

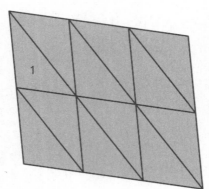

Quadrilaterals

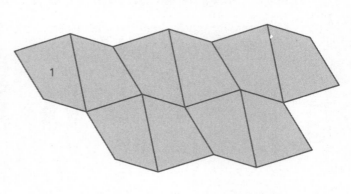

 b. **EXPERIMENT** Will *any* triangle tessellate? Conduct an experiment to
   gather information to help form your conclusion. Draw a triangle. Cut it
   out. Then use it to trace other triangles so that you cover the plane with
   triangles that are all the same shape.

5.7 **Rotations** (continued)

c. **EXPERIMENT** Will *any* quadrilateral tessellate? Conduct an experiment to gather information to help form your conclusion. Draw a quadrilateral. Cut it out. Then use it to trace other quadrilaterals so that you cover the plane with quadrilaterals that are all the same shape.

What Is Your Answer?

3. **IN YOUR OWN WORDS** What are the three basic ways to move an object in a plane? Draw an example of each.

"Dear Sub Shop: Why do you put the cheese on the subs so some parts have double coverage and some have none?"

"My suggestion is that you use the tessellation property of triangles for even cheese coverage."

Name _____ Date _____

Tell whether the shaded figure is a rotation of the nonshaded figure about the origin. If so, give the angle and the direction of rotation.

1.
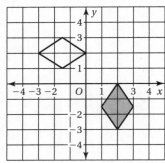

2.
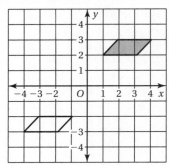

The vertices of a triangle are $A(1, 1)$, $B(3, 1)$, and $C(3, 4)$. Rotate the triangle as described. Find the coordinates of the image.

3. 90° clockwise about the origin

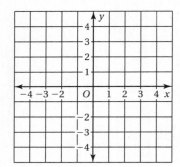

4. 270° counterclockwise about vertex A

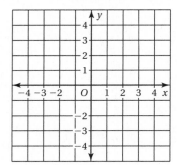

5. A triangle is rotated 180° about the origin. Its image is reflected in the x-axis. The vertices of the final triangle are $(-4, -4)$, $(-2, -4)$, and $(-3, -1)$. What are the vertices of the original triangle?

Name_____ Date_____

Find the area.

1.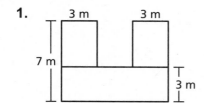

2.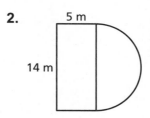

3.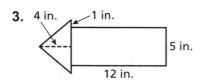

4.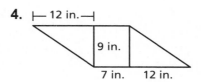

5.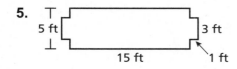

6.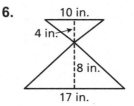

7. You are putting carpet in 2 rooms of your house. The carpet costs $1.48 per square foot. How much does it cost to put carpet in the rooms?

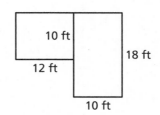

Chapter 6 **Fair Game Review** (continued)

Find the area.

8.
20 in.

9.
6 m

10.
12 cm

11.
14 ft

12.
25 yd

13.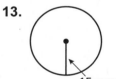
15 mm

14. Find the area of the shaded region.

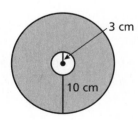
3 cm

10 cm

Drawing 3-Dimensional Figures
For use with Activity 6.1

Essential Question How can you draw three-dimensional figures?

1 **ACTIVITY:** Finding Surface Area and Volumes

Work with a partner.

Draw the front, side, and top views of each stack of cubes. Then find the surface area and volume. Each small cube has side lengths of 1 unit.

a.
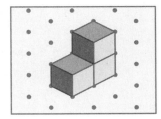
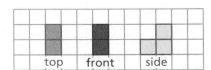

b.  c.  d.

e.  f. 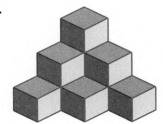 g.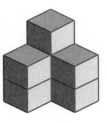

6.1 Drawing 3-Dimensional Figures (continued)

2 ACTIVITY: Drawing Solids

Work with a partner.

a. Draw all the different solids you can make by joining four cubes. (Two have been drawn.) Cubes must be joined on faces, not on edges only. Translations, reflections, and rotations do not count as different solids.

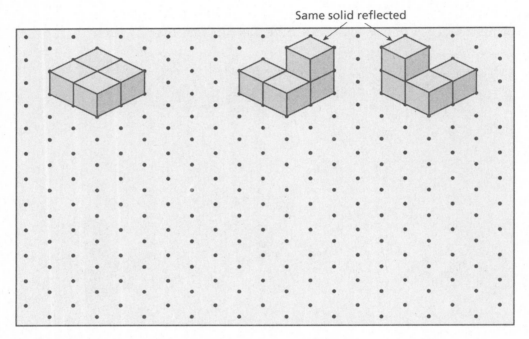

Same solid reflected

b. Do all the solids have the same surface area? Do all the solids have the same volume? Explain your reasoning.

6.1 **Drawing 3-Dimensional Figures** (continued)

What Is Your Answer?

3. **IN YOUR OWN WORDS** How can you draw three-dimensional figures? Draw and shade two prisms that have the same volume but different surface areas.

4. Maurits Escher (1898–1972) was a popular artist who drew optical illusions.

   a. What is the illusion in Escher's drawing?

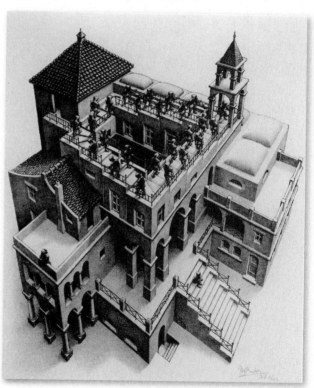

© 2008 M.C. Escher's "Ascending and Descending"

   b. Why is the cartoon funny? What is the illusion in the cartoon?

6.1 **Practice**
For use after Lesson 6.1

Draw the solid.

1. Pentagonal pyramid

2. Square prism

Draw the front, side, and top views of the solid.

3.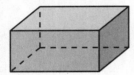

4.

5. Two of the three views of a solid are shown.

   a. What is the greatest number of unit cubes in the solid?

   Front   Side

   b. Draw the top view of the solid in part (a).

6. Draw a solid with the following front, side, and top views.

   Front   Side   Top

6.2 Surface Areas of Prisms
For use with Activity 6.2

Essential Question How can you use a net to find the surface area of a prism?

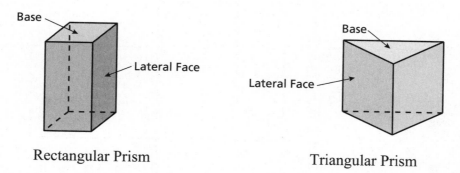

Rectangular Prism   Triangular Prism

The **surface area** of a prism is the sum of the areas of all its faces. A two-dimensional representation of a solid is called a **net**.

1 ACTIVITY: Surface Area of a Right Rectangular Prism

Work with a partner.

a. Use the net for the rectangular prism to find its surface area.

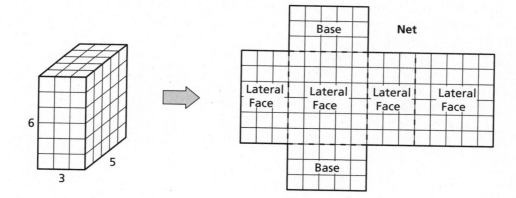

6.2 **Surface Areas of Prisms** (continued)

b. Use the net for a rectangular prism. Label each side as h, w, or ℓ. Then write a formula for the surface area of a rectangular prism.

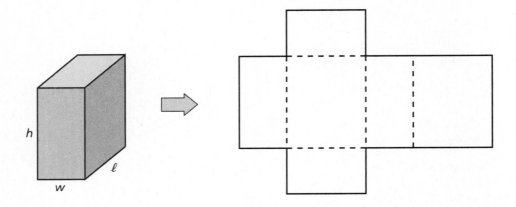

---

2 ACTIVITY: Finding Surface Area

Work with a partner. Find the surface area of the solid shown by the net. Use a cut-out of the net.* Fold it to form a solid. Identify the solid.

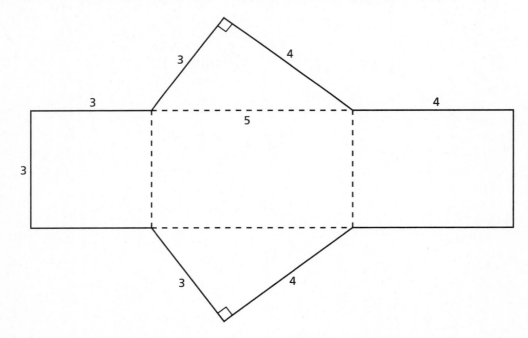

*Cut-outs are available in the back of the Record and Practice Journal.

6.2 **Surface Areas of Prisms** (continued)

What Is Your Answer?

3. **IN YOUR OWN WORDS** How can you use a net to find the surface area of a prism? Draw a net, cut it out, and fold it to form a prism.

4. The greater the surface area of an ice block, the faster it will melt. Which will melt faster, the bigger block or the three smaller blocks? Explain your reasoning.

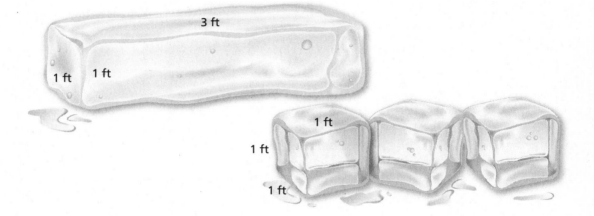

Name _____ Date _____

Draw a net for the prism. Then find the surface area.

1.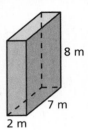
8 m
7 m
2 m

2.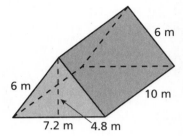
6 m
6 m
10 m
7.2 m   4.8 m

Find the surface area of the prism.

3.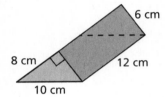
6 cm
8 cm   12 cm
10 cm

4.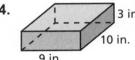
3 in.
10 in.
9 in.

5. You bake a 9-inch by 13-inch by 2-inch cake. Your frosting recipe makes enough to cover 250 square inches of cake. Do you have enough frosting? (Assume you do not need to frost the bottom of the cake.) Explain your reasoning.

6. You buy a ring box as a birthday gift that is in the shape of a triangular prism. What is the least amount of wrapping paper needed to wrap the box?

14.5 cm
8 cm
10 cm   10.5 cm

6.3 Surface Areas of Cylinders
For use with Activity 6.3

Essential Question How can you find the surface area of a cylinder?

---

1 ACTIVITY: Finding Area

Work with a partner. Use a cardboard cylinder.

- **Talk about how you can find the area of the outside of the roll.**

- **Use a ruler to estimate the area of the outside of the roll.**

- **Cut the roll and press it out flat. Then find the area of the flattened cardboard. How close is your estimate to the actual area?**

Cut

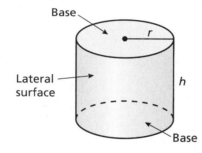

Base

r

Lateral surface

h

Base

The surface area of a cylinder is the sum of the areas of the bases and the lateral surface.

---

2 ACTIVITY: Finding Surface Area

Work with a partner.

- **Trace the top and bottom of a can on paper. Cut out the two shapes.**

- **Cut out a long paper rectangle. Make the width the same as the height of the can. Wrap the rectangle around the can. Cut off the excess paper so the edges just meet.**

- **Make a net for the can. Name the shapes in the net.**

6.3 **Surface Areas of Cylinders** (continued)

- How are the dimensions of the rectangle related to the dimensions of the can?

- Explain how to use the net to find the surface area of the can.

---

3 **ACTIVITY:** Estimation

Work with a partner. From memory, estimate the dimensions of the real-life items in parts (a)–(d) in inches. Then use the dimensions to estimate the surface area of each item in square inches.

a.

b.

6.3 **Surface Areas of Cylinders** (continued)

c.

d.

What Is Your Answer?

4. IN YOUR OWN WORDS How can you find the surface area of a cylinder? Give an example with your description. Include a drawing of the cylinder.

5. To eight decimal places, $\pi \approx 3.14159265$. Which of the following is closest to π?

a. 3.14   **b.** $\dfrac{22}{7}$ **c.** $\dfrac{355}{113}$

"To approximate the irrational number $\pi \approx 3.141593$, I simply remember 1, 1, 3, 3, 5, 5."

"Then I compute the rational number $\frac{355}{113} \approx 3.141593$."

6.3 Practice
For use after Lesson 6.3

Find the surface area of the cylinder. Round your answer to the nearest tenth.

1.
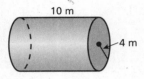
10 m

4 m

2.
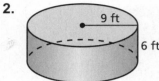
9 ft

6 ft

Find the lateral surface area of the cylinder. Round your answer to the nearest tenth.

3.
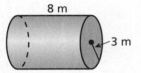
8 m

3 m

4.
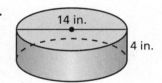
14 in.

4 in.

5. How much paper is used in the label for the can of cat food? Round your answer to the nearest whole number.

30 mm

24 mm

6. The circumference of a base of a cylinder is 33.3 inches and the height of the cylinder is 7.7 inches. What is the surface area of the cylinder?

6.4 Surface Areas of Pyramids
For use with Activity 6.4

Essential Question How can you find the surface area of a pyramid?

Even though many well-known **pyramids** have square bases, the base of a pyramid can be any polygon.

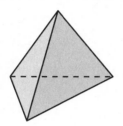

Triangular Base

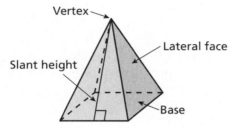

Vertex

Slant height

Lateral face

Base

Square Base

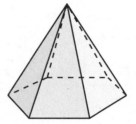

Hexagonal Base

1 ACTIVITY: Making a Scale Model

Work with a partner. Each pyramid has a square base.

- **Draw a net for a scale model of one of the pyramids. Describe your scale.**
- **Cut out the net and fold it to form a pyramid.**
- **Find the lateral surface area of the real-life pyramid.**

a. Cheops Pyramid in Egypt
Side = 230 m, Slant height ≈ 186 m

b. Muttart Conservatory in Edmonton
Side = 26 m, Slant height ≈ 27 m

c. Louvre Pyramid in Paris
Side = 35 m, Slant height ≈ 28 m

d. Pyramid of Caius Cestius in Rome
Side = 22 m, Slant height ≈ 29 m

6.4   Surface Areas of Pyramids (continued)

2   ACTIVITY: Estimation

Work with a partner. There are many different types of gemstone cuts. Here is one called a brilliant cut.

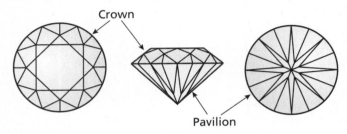

Top View   *Side View*   *Bottom View*

Crown

Pavilion

The size and shape of the pavilion can be approximated by an octagonal pyramid.

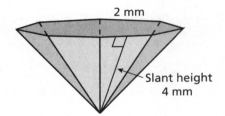

2 mm

Slant height
4 mm

a. What does octagonal mean?

b. Draw a net for the pyramid.

c. Find the lateral surface area of the pyramid.

6.4 **Surface Areas of Pyramids** (continued)

---

3 **ACTIVITY:** Building a Skylight

Work with a partner. The skylight has 12 triangular pieces of glass. Each piece has a base of 1 foot and a slant height of 3 feet.

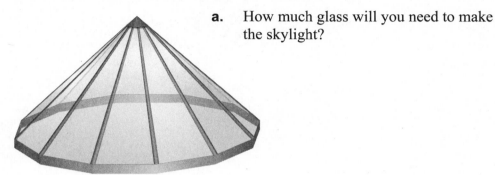

a. How much glass will you need to make the skylight?

b. Can you cut the 12 glass triangles from a sheet of glass that is 4 feet by 8 feet? If so, draw a diagram showing how this can be done.

What Is Your Answer?

4. IN YOUR OWN WORDS How can you find the surface area of a pyramid? Draw a diagram with your explanation.

Name _____ Date _____

Find the surface area of the regular pyramid.

1.

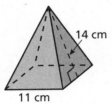

14 cm

11 cm

2.

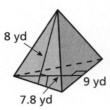

8 yd

9 yd

7.8 yd

3.

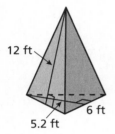

12 ft

6 ft

5.2 ft

4.

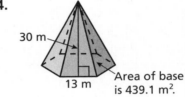

30 m

13 m

Area of base
is 439.1 m².

5. The surface area of a triangular pyramid is 305 square inches. The area of the base is 35 square inches. Each face has a base of 9 inches. What is the slant height?

6. A candle shaped like a square pyramid needs wrapped in paper. How much paper is needed to cover a candle that has a base side of 6 centimeters and a slant height of 10 centimeters?

6.5 Surface Areas of Cones
For use with Activity 6.5

Essential Question How can you find the surface area of a cone?

A cone is a solid with one circular base and one vertex.

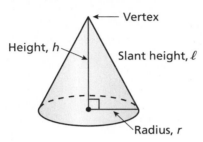

1 ACTIVITY: Finding the Surface Area of a Cone

Work with a partner.

- **Draw a circle with a radius of 3 inches.***

- **Mark the circumference of the circle into six equal parts.**

- **The circumference of the circle is $2(\pi)(3) = 6\pi$. So each of the six parts on the circle has a length of π. Label each part.**

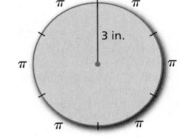

- **Cut one part as shown. Then, make a cone.**

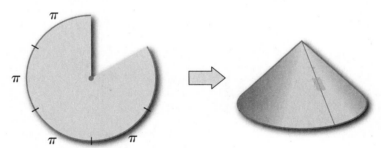

a. The base of the cone should be a circle. Explain why the circumference of the base is 5π.

b. Find the radius of the base.

*Cut-outs are available in the back of the Record and Practice Journal.

6.5 **Surface Areas of Cones** (continued)

    c. What is the area of the original circle?

    d. What is the area of the circle with one part missing?

    e. Describe the surface area of the cone. Use your description to find the surface area, including the base.

2 **ACTIVITY:** Experimenting with Surface Area

Work with a partner.

- **Cut out another part from the circle in Activity 1 and make a cone.**
- **Find the radius of the base and the surface area of the cone.**
- **Record your results in the table.**
- **Repeat this three times.**
- **Describe the pattern.**

Shape					
Radius of Base					
Slant Height					
Surface Area					

6.5 **Surface Areas of Cones** (continued)

3 **ACTIVITY:** Writing a Story

Write a story that uses real-life cones. Include a diagram and label the dimensions. In your story, explain why you would want to know the surface area of the cone. Then estimate the surface area.

What Is Your Answer?

4. **IN YOUR OWN WORDS** How can you find the surface area of a cone? Draw a diagram with your explanation.

Name _____ Date _____

Find the surface area of the cone. Round your answer to the nearest tenth.

1.

2.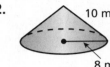

Find the slant height ℓ of the cone.

3. $S = 112\pi$ ft^2

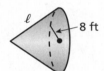

4. $S = 108\pi$ in.^{2}

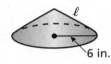

5. A cone-shaped container to hold balloons has a diameter of 2 inches and a slant height of 4 inches. How much paper is needed to wrap the container? Round your answer to the nearest tenth.

6. For a children's play, you design a hat shaped like a cone for a princess. The hat has a radius of 4 inches and a slant height of 2 feet. How much material do you need to make the hat? Round your answer to the nearest tenth.

6.6 Surface Areas of Composite Solids
For use with Activity 6.6

Essential Question How can you find the surface area of a composite solid?

1 **ACTIVITY:** Finding a Surface Area

Work with a partner. You are manufacturing scale models of old houses.

a. Name the four basic solids in this composite figure.

b. Determine a strategy for finding the surface area of this model. Would you use a scale drawing? Would you use a net? Explain.

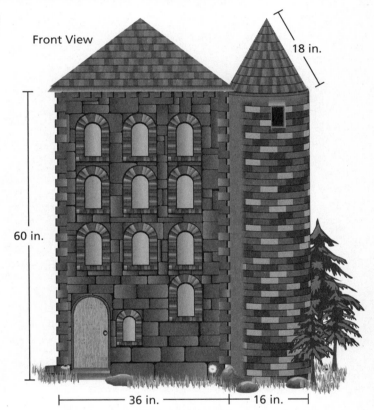

Front View

60 in.

36 in.   16 in.

18 in.

Many castles have cylindrical towers with conical roofs. These are called turrets.

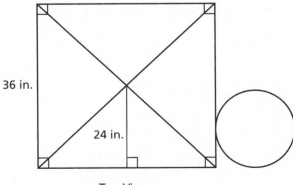

36 in.

24 in.

Top View

6.6 Surface Areas of Composite Solids (continued)

2 ACTIVITY: Finding and Using a Pattern

Work with a partner.

- **Find the surface area of each figure.**

- **Use a table to organize your results.**

- **Describe the pattern in the table.**

- **Use the pattern to find the surface area of the figure that has a base of 10 blocks.**

3 ACTIVITY: Finding and Using a Pattern

Work with a partner. You own a roofing company. Each building has the same base area. Which roof would be cheapest? Which would be the most expensive? Explain your reasoning.

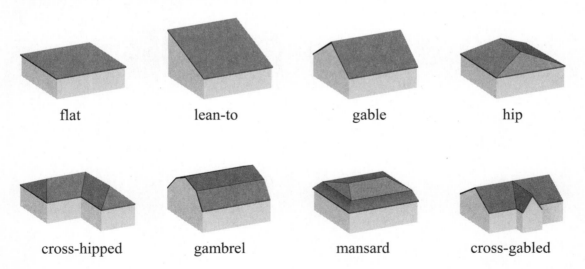

flat   lean-to   gable   hip

cross-hipped   gambrel   mansard   cross-gabled

6.6 **Surface Areas of Composite Solids** (continued)

What Is Your Answer?

4. **IN YOUR OWN WORDS** How can you find the surface area of a composite solid?

5. Design a building that has a turret and also has a mansard roof. Find the surface area of the roof.

6.6 Practice

For use after Lesson 6.6

Identify the solids that form the composite solid. Then find the surface area. Round your answer to the nearest tenth.

1.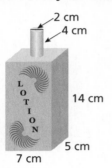

2 cm
4 cm
14 cm
5 cm
7 cm

2.

100 mm   10 mm
GRAY
20 mm

3.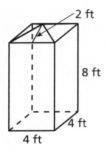

2 ft
8 ft
4 ft
4 ft

4.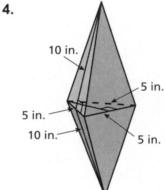

10 in.
5 in.
5 in.
10 in.
5 in.

5. The block is made up of a cylinder and a prism. What is the surface area of the block? Round your answer to the nearest tenth.

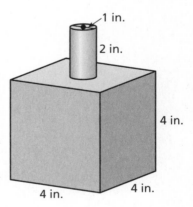

1 in.
2 in.
4 in.
4 in.
4 in.

Chapter 7 **Fair Game Review**

Tell whether the figures are similar. Explain your reasoning.

1.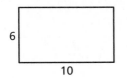

2.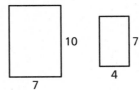

3.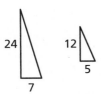

4.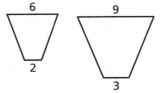

5.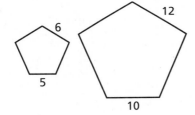

6.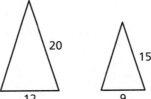

7. Two mirrors are hung on a wall. The large mirror has a length of 3 feet and width of 2 feet. The smaller mirror has a length of 1 foot and width of 6 inches. Are the figures similar? Explain your reasoning.

Chapter 7 **Fair Game Review** (continued)

The figures are similar. Find the value of x.

8.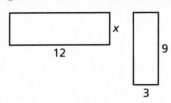

9.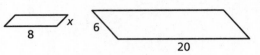

10.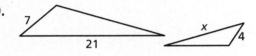

11.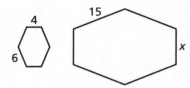

12.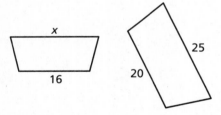

13.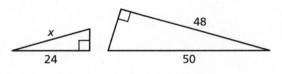

14. The front door of your house is similar to the front door of a dollhouse. The door to your house is 8 feet long and 3.5 feet wide. The dollhouse door is 6 inches long. How wide is the dollhouse door?

Name_____ Date _____

Essential Question How can you find the volume of a prism?

1 ACTIVITY: Pearls in a Treasure Chest

Work with a partner. A treasure chest is filled with valuable pearls. Each pearl is about 1 centimeter in diameter and is worth about $80.

Use the diagrams below to describe two ways that you can estimate the number of pearls in the treasure chest.

a.

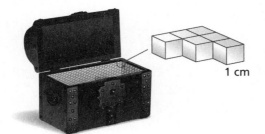

1 cm

120 cm

60 cm

60 cm

b.

c. Use the method in part (a) to estimate the value of the pearls in the chest.

7.1 **Volumes of Prisms** (continued)

---

2 **ACTIVITY:** Finding a Formula for Volume

Work with a partner. You know that the formula for the volume of a rectangular prism is $V = \ell wh$.

    a. Find a new formula that gives the volume in terms of the area of the base B and the height h.

    b. Use both formulas to find the volume of each prism. Do both formulas give you the same volumes?

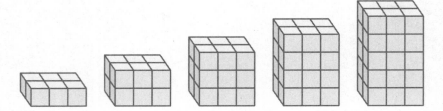

---

3 **ACTIVITY:** Finding a Formula for Volume

Work with a partner. Use the concept in Activity 2 to find a formula that gives the volume of any prism.

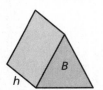

Triangular Prism

Rectangular Prism

Pentagonal Prism

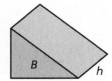

Triangular Prism

Hexagonal Prism

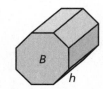

Octagonal Prism

7.1 Volumes of Prisms (continued)

4 **ACTIVITY:** Using a Formula

Work with a partner. A ream of paper has 500 sheets.

  a. Does a single sheet of paper have a volume? Why or why not?

  b. If so, explain how you can find the volume of a single piece of paper.

What Is Your Answer?

  5. IN YOUR OWN WORDS How can you find the volume of a prism?

  6. Draw a prism that has a trapezoid as its base. Use your formula to find the volume of the prism.

Practice
For use after Lesson 7.1

Find the volume of the prism.

1.
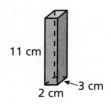
3 in.
4 in.
5 in.

2.
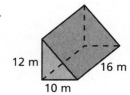
12 m
16 m
10 m

3.
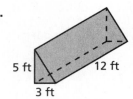
5 ft
12 ft
3 ft

4.
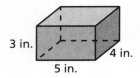
11 cm
2 cm
3 cm

5. $B = 60 \text{ ft}^2$
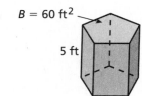
5 ft

6. $B = 80 \text{ m}^2$
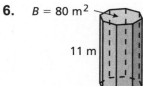
11 m

7.   Each box is shaped like a rectangular prism. Which has more storage space? Explain.

Box 1
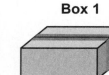
5 in.
8 in.
12 in.

Box 2
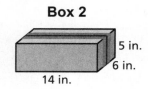
5 in.
6 in.
14 in.

7.2 Volumes of Cylinders
For use with Activity 7.2

Essential Question How can you find the volume of a cylinder?

1 ACTIVITY: Finding a Formula Experimentally

Work with a partner.

a. Find the area of the face of a coin.

b. Find the volume of a stack of a dozen coins.

c. Generalize your results to find the volume of a cylinder.

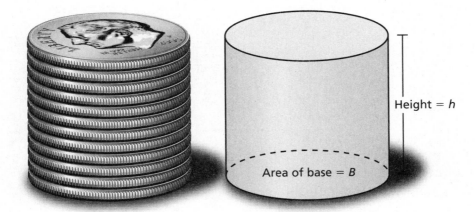

Height = *h*

Area of base = *B*

7.2 **Volumes of Cylinders** (continued)

2 **ACTIVITY:** Making a Business Plan

Work with a partner. You are planning to make and sell 3 different sizes of cylindrical candles. You buy 1 cubic foot of candle wax for $20 to make 8 candles of each size.

a. Design the candles. What are the dimensions of each size?

b. You want to make a profit of $100. Decide on a price for each size.

c. Did you set the prices so that they are proportional to the volume of each size of candle? Why or why not?

3 **ACTIVITY:** Science Experiment

Work with a partner. Use the diagram to describe how you can find the volume of a small object.

7.2 **Volumes of Cylinders** (continued)

4 **ACTIVITY:** Comparing Cylinders

Work with a partner.

a. Just by looking at two cylinders, which one do you think has the greater volume? Explain your reasoning.

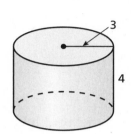 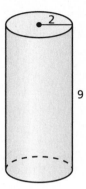

b. Find the volume of each cylinder. Was your prediction in part (a) correct? Explain your reasoning.

What Is Your Answer?

5. **IN YOUR OWN WORDS** How can you find the volume of a cylinder?

6. Compare your formula for the volume of a cylinder with the formula for the volume of a prism. How are they the same?

7.2 Practice
For use after Lesson 7.2

Find the volume of the cylinder. Round your answer to the nearest tenth.

1.

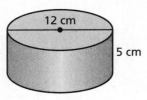

12 cm

5 cm

2. 4 in.

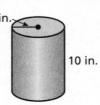

10 in.

Find the height of the cylinder. Round your answer to the nearest whole number.

3. Volume = 84 in.³

6 in.

4. Volume = 650 cm³

8 cm

5. What happens to the volume of a cylinder if you double the radius?

6. To make orange juice, the directions call for a can of orange juice concentrate to be mixed with three cans of water. What is the volume of orange juice that you make?

3 in.

Orange Juice

5 in.

7.3 Volumes of Pyramids
For use with Activity 7.3

Essential Question How can you find the volume of a pyramid?

---

1 ACTIVITY: Finding a Formula Experimentally

Work with a partner.

- **Draw the two nets on cardboard and cut them out.***

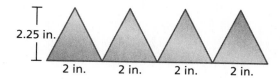

2.25 in.

2 in.   2 in.   2 in.   2 in.

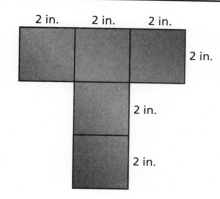

2 in.   2 in.   2 in.

2 in.

2 in.

2 in.

- **Fold and tape the nets to form an open square box and an open pyramid.**

- **Both figures should have the same size square base and the same height.**

- **Fill the pyramid with pebbles. Then pour the pebbles into the box. Repeat this until the box is full. How many pyramids does it take to fill the box?**

- **Use your result to find a formula for the volume of a pyramid.**

---

2 ACTIVITY: Comparing Volumes

Work with a partner. You are an archeologist studying two ancient pyramids. What factors would affect how long it took to build each pyramid? Given similar conditions, which pyramid took longer to build? Explain your reasoning.

Cholula Pyramid in Mexico
Height: about 217 ft
Base: about 1476 ft by 1476 ft

Cheops Pyramid in Egypt
Height: about 480 ft
Base: about 755 ft by 755 ft

*Cut-outs are available in the back of the Record and Practice Journal.

7.3 **Volumes of Pyramids** (continued)

3 **ACTIVITY:** Finding and Using a Pattern

Work with a partner.

- **Find the volumes of the pyramids.**

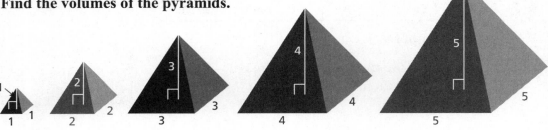

- **Organize your results in a table.**

- **Describe the pattern.**

_____

- **Use your pattern to find the volume of a pyramid with a side length and height of 20.**

7.3 Volumes of Pyramids (continued)

4 ACTIVITY: Breaking a Prism into Pyramids

Work with a partner. The rectangular prism can be cut to form three pyramids. Show that the sum of the volumes of the three pyramids is equal to the volume of the prism.

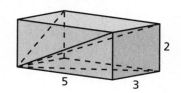

a.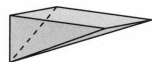

b.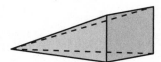

c.

What Is Your Answer?

5. **IN YOUR OWN WORDS** How can you find the volume of a pyramid?

6. Write a general formula for the volume of a pyramid.

7.3 **Practice**
For use after Lesson 7.3

Find the volume of the pyramid.

1.

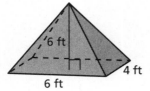

6 ft

6 ft

4 ft

6 ft

2.

10 yd

9 yd

8 yd

3.

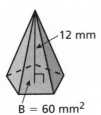

12 mm

B = 60 mm²

4.

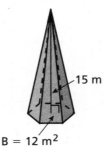

15 m

B = 12 m²

5. You create a simple tent in the shape of a pyramid. What is the volume of the tent?

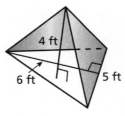

4 ft

6 ft

5 ft

6. You work at a restaurant that has 20 tables. Each table has a set of salt and pepper shakers on it that are in the shape of square pyramids. How much salt do you need to fill all the salt shakers?

3 in.

2 in.   2 in.

7.4 **Volumes of Cones**
For use with Activity 7.4

Essential Question How can you remember the formulas for surface area and volume?

You discovered that the volume of a pyramid is one-third the volume of a prism that has the same base and same height. You can use a similar activity to discover that the volume of a cone is one-third the volume of a cylinder that has the same base and height.

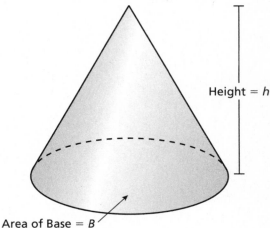

Height = h

Area of Base = B

Volume of a Cone = $\frac{1}{3}$(Area of Base) $\times$ (Height)

1 **ACTIVITY:** Summarizing Volume Formulas

Work with a partner. You can remember the volume formulas for all of the solids shown with just two concepts.

Volumes of Prisms and Cylinders

Volume = (Area of Base) $\times$ (Height)

Volumes of Pyramids and Cones

Volume = $\frac{1}{3}$(Volume of Prism or Cylinder with same base and height)

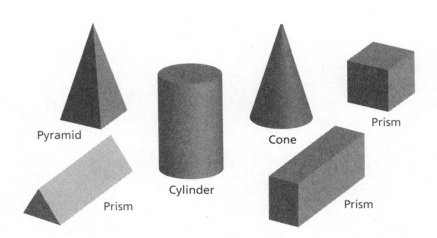

Pyramid

Prism

Cylinder

Cone

Prism

Prism

7.4 Volumes of Cones (continued)

Make a list of all the formulas you need to remember to find the area of
a base. Talk about strategies for remembering these formulas.

---

2 **ACTIVITY:** Volumes of Oblique Solids

Work with a partner. Think of a stack of paper. If you adjust the stack so
that the sides are oblique (slanted), do you change the volume of the stack?
If the volume of the stack does not change, then the formulas for volumes
of right solids also apply to oblique solids.

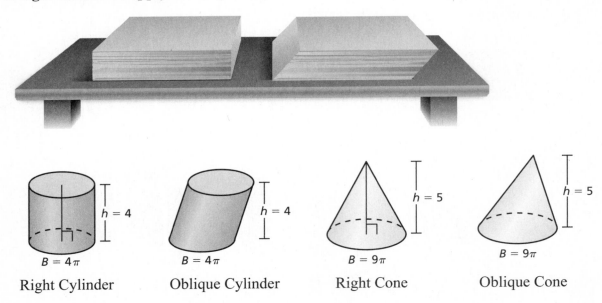

Right Cylinder   Oblique Cylinder   Right Cone   Oblique Cone

7.4 Volumes of Cones (continued)

3 **ACTIVITY:** Summarizing Surface Area Formulas

Work with a partner. Make a list of the formulas for surface area that you studied in Chapter 6. Organize these formulas in a way similar to what you did in Activity 1.

Surface Area of a Right Prism =

Surface Area of a Right Pyramid =

Surface Area of a Right Cylinder =

Surface Area of a Right Cone =

What Is Your Answer?

4. **IN YOUR OWN WORDS** How can you remember the formulas for surface area and volume? Write all of the surface area and volume formulas on a summary sheet. Make the list short so that you do not have to memorize many formulas.

Name _____ Date _____

Find the volume of the cone. Round your answer to the nearest tenth.

1.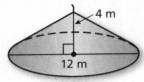
4 m
12 m

2.
3 ft
11 ft

3.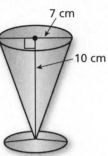
7 cm
10 cm

Find the height of the cone. Round your answer to the nearest tenth.

4. Volume $= 300\pi$ mm^3

5. Volume $= 78.5$ cm^3

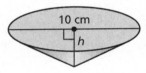
h
12 mm

10 cm
h

6. What is the volume of the catch and click cone?

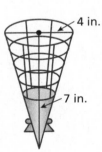
4 in.
7 in.

7. You have a candle mold that creates candles like the one shown. How many candles can you make with 170 cubic inches of candle wax?

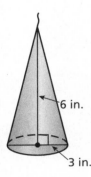
6 in.
3 in.

7.5 Volumes of Composite Solids
For use with Activity 7.5

Essential Question   How can you estimate the volume of a composite solid?

1   ACTIVITY: Estimating Volume

Work with a partner. You work for a toy company and need to estimate the volume of a Minifigure that will be modeled out of plastic.

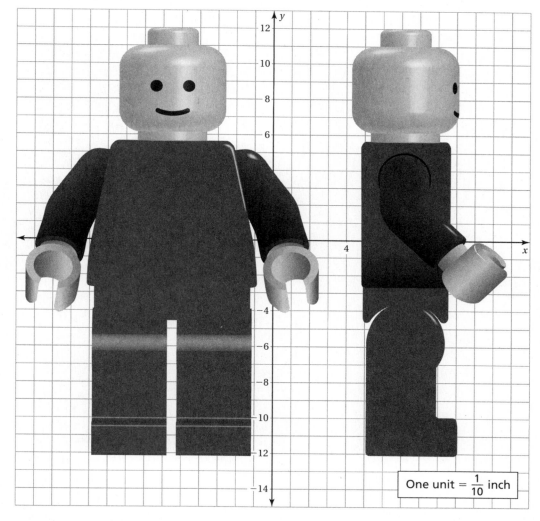

One unit = $\frac{1}{10}$ inch

a. Estimate the number of cubic inches of plastic that is needed to mold the Minifigure's head. Show your work.

7.5 **Volumes of Composite Solids** (continued)

b. Estimate the number of cubic inches of plastic that is needed to mold one of the Minifigure's legs. Show your work.

2 **ACTIVITY:** Finding the Volumes of Composite Solids

Work with a partner.

a. Make a plan for estimating the amount of plastic it takes to make a standard eight-stud LEGO® Brick.

$\frac{5}{8}$ in. $\frac{5}{4}$ in. $\frac{3}{16}$ in.

$\frac{3}{8}$ in. $\frac{1}{16}$ in.

7.5 **Volumes of Composite Solids** (continued)

b. How much water, in cubic inches, would it take to make ten
LEGO® Brick ice cubes?

What Is Your Answer?

3. IN YOUR OWN WORDS How can you estimate the volume of a composite
solid? Try thinking of some alternative strategies.

7.5 Practice
For use after Lesson 7.5

Find the volume of the composite solid. Round your answer to the nearest tenth.

1.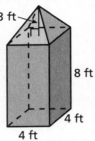
3 ft
8 ft
4 ft
4 ft

2.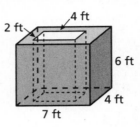
4 ft
2 ft
6 ft
4 ft
7 ft

3.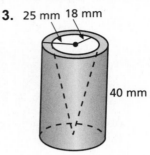
25 mm   18 mm
40 mm

4. An ornament is made up of two identical square pyramids. Find the volume of the ornament.

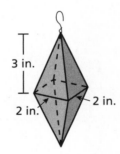
3 in.
2 in.
2 in.

5. An angel food cake pan is shown. What is the volume of the pan? Round your answer to the nearest tenth.

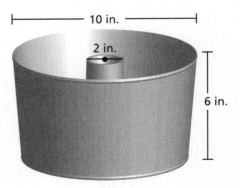
10 in.
2 in.
6 in.

7.6 Surface Areas and Volumes of Similar Solids
For use with Activity 7.6

Essential Question When the dimensions of a solid increase by a factor of k, how does the surface area change? How does the volume change?

1 ACTIVITY: Comparing Volumes and Surface Areas

Work with a partner. Complete the table. Describe the pattern. Are the solids similar? Explain your reasoning.

a.

Radius	1	1	1	1	1
Height	1	2	3	4	5
Surface Area					
Volume					

7.6 Surface Areas and Volumes of Similar Solids (continued)

b.

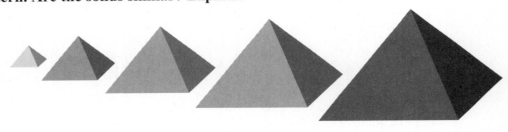

Radius	1	2	3	4	5
Height	1	2	3	4	5
Surface Area					
Volume					

2 **ACTIVITY:** Comparing Volumes and Surface Areas

Work with a partner. Complete the table. Describe the pattern. Are the solids similar? Explain.

Base Side	6	12	18	24	30
Height	4	8	12	16	20
Slant Height	5	10	15	20	25
Surface Area					
Volume					

7.6 **Surface Areas and Volumes of Similar Solids** (continued)

What Is Your Answer?

3. **IN YOUR OWN WORDS** When the dimensions of a solid increase by a factor of k, how does the surface area change?

4. **IN YOUR OWN WORDS** When the dimensions of a solid increase by a factor of k, how does the volume change?

5. All the dimensions of a cone increase by a factor of 5.

   a. How many times greater is the surface area? Explain.

    | 5 | 10 | 25 | 125 |

   b. How many times greater is the volume? Explain.

    | 5 | 10 | 25 | 125 |

Name _____ Date _____

Determine whether the solids are similar.

1.

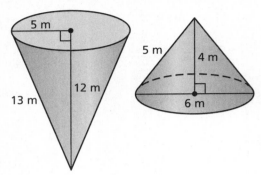

5 m

5 m   4 m

12 m

13 m   6 m

2.

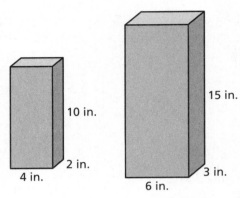

10 in.

15 in.

2 in.

4 in.   6 in.   3 in.

The solids are similar. Find the missing dimension(s).

3.

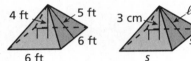

4 ft   5 ft   3 cm   ℓ

6 ft   s

6 ft   s

4.

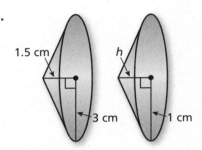

1.5 cm   h

3 cm   1 cm

The solids are similar. Find the surface area S or volume V of the shaded solid.

5.

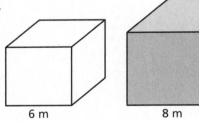

6 m   8 m

Surface Area = 198 m²

6.

Volume = 54 mm³

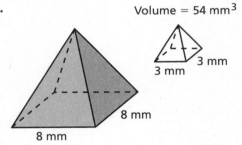

3 mm   3 mm

8 mm   8 mm

8 mm

7. A type of tomato sauce is offered in two sizes. Are the cans similar? Explain.

3 in.   4 in.

Tomato Sauce   Tomato Sauce

5 in.   6 in.

Name_____ Date _____

  Fair Game Review

Chapter 8

Use the data set to find the (a) mean, (b) median, (c) mode(s),
and (d) range.

1.

Player	A	B	C	D
Blocks	8	3	6	3

2.

Phone Plan	A	B	C	D
Minutes	200	400	700	2000

3.

Meeting	Jan	Feb	Mar	Apr	May
People	13	19	24	15	19

4.

Customer	A	B	C	D	E	F
Donation	10	20	25	10	50	20

5.

Day	M	T	W	Th	F
Emails	8	10	6	11	7

6.

Day	Su	M	T	W	Th	F	Sa
Hours	3	3	5	2	3	1	0

Fair Game Review (continued)

7. The data show your bowling scores for four games. What is the mean, median, mode, and range of your scores?

Game	Score
1	89
2	102
3	112
4	109

8. The data in the table shows the scores on a recent test.

   a. Find the mean, median, mode(s), and range.

Test Scores		
91	96	82
84	84	78
77	72	99
79	95	92
74	71	70
88	83	79

   b. What is the best way to measure the data?

   c. Two students have yet to take the test. How can their scores change your answers to parts (a) and (b)?

8.1 Stem-and-Leaf Plots
For use with Activity 8.1

Essential Question How can you use a stem-and-leaf plot to organize a set of numbers?

---

1 ACTIVITY: Decoding a Graph

Work with a partner. You intercept a secret message that contains two different types of plots. You suspect that each plot represents the same data. The graph with the dots indicates only ranges for the numbers.

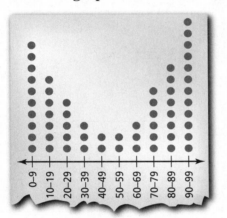

0	0 1 2 2 3 4 4 7 8 9
1	2 2 5 6 7 8 9
2	2 2 6 8 9
3	5 8 9
4	2 7
5	4 5
6	2 7 8
7	2 3 6 7 9 9
8	2 2 4 5 5 6 8 9
9	1 1 1 1 1 2 2 2 2 3 3

a. How many numbers are in the data set? How can you tell?

b. How many numbers are greater than or equal to 90? How can you tell?

c. Is 91 in the data set? If so, how many times is it in the set? How can you tell?

d. Make a list of all the numbers in the data set.

8.1 Stem-and-Leaf Plots (continued)

e. You intercept a new secret message. Use the secret code shown below to decode the message.

Secret Code

A = 29	F = 31	K = 18	P = 4	U = 19
B = 33	G = 8	L = 26	Q = 10	V = 17
C = 7	H = 16	M = 22	R = 21	W = 12
D = 20	I = 5	N = 3	S = 2	X = 25
E = 15	J = 11	O = 9	T = 32	Y = 13
				Z = 1

$\overline{32}\ \overline{16}\ \overline{15}$ $\overline{2}\ \overline{32}\ \overline{15}\ \overline{22}$ $\overline{2}\ \overline{16}\ \overline{9}\ \overline{12}\ \overline{2}$ $\overline{32}\ \overline{16}\ \overline{15}$ $\overline{32}\ \overline{15}\ \overline{3}\ \overline{2}$

$\overline{32}\ \overline{16}\ \overline{15}$ $\overline{26}\ \overline{15}\ \overline{29}\ \overline{17}\ \overline{15}\ \overline{2}$ $\overline{2}\ \overline{16}\ \overline{9}\ \overline{12}$ $\overline{32}\ \overline{16}\ \overline{15}$ $\overline{9}\ \overline{3}\ \overline{15}\ \overline{2}$

---

2 ACTIVITY: Organizing Data

Work with a partner. You are working on an archeological dig. You find several arrowheads. As you find each arrowhead, you measure its length (in millimeters) and record it in a notebook.

18	61	62
42	42	42
23	41	40
45	45	45
37	28	50
35	39	34
37	32	26
63	24	54
58	58	60
52	53	72
17	73	

a. Use a stem-and-leaf plot to organize the lengths.

b. Find the mean length.

c. Find the median length.

d. Describe the distribution of the data.

8.1 **Stem-and-Leaf Plots** (continued)

3 **ACTIVITY:** Conducting an Experiment

Work with a partner. Use two number cubes to conduct the following experiment.

- **Toss the cubes four times and total the results.**

  Sample: $2 + 3 + 2 + 2 + 3 + 5 + 6 + 3 = 26$ So, 26 is the

  1st toss   2nd toss   3rd toss   4th toss   first number.

- **Repeat this process 29 more times.**

- **Use a stem-and-leaf plot to organize your results.**

- **Describe your results.**

What Is Your Answer?

4. **IN YOUR OWN WORDS** How can you use a stem-and-leaf plot to organize a set of numbers?

5. **RESEARCH** Find a career in which a person collects and organizes data. Describe how data are collected and organized in that career.

8.1 Practice
For use after Lesson 8.1

Make a stem-and-leaf plot of the data.

1.

Class Sizes			
12	10	21	28
9	16	19	16
25	32	14	21

2.

Minutes Spent on Homework			
75	82	91	68
92	86	79	76
75	81	88	60

3. The number of text messages from eight phones are 8, 11, 14, 22, 5, 15, 7, and 20. Make a stem-and-leaf plot of the data. Describe the distribution of the data.

4. The number of minutes seven members spent at band practice are 57, 49, 55, 62, 78, 72, and 75. Make a stem-and-leaf plot of the data. Describe the distribution of the data.

5. The stem-and-leaf plot shows the number of miles students travel to get to school.

    a. How many students travel more than 15 miles?

    b. Find the mean, median, mode, and range of the data.

Stem	Leaf
0	5 7
1	2 4 8
2	0 1 5 7
3	3

Key: 1 | 4 = 14 miles

8.2 Histograms
For use with Activity 8.2

Essential Question   How do histograms show the differences in distributions of data?

1 ACTIVITY: Analyzing Distributions

Work with a partner. The graphs (histograms) show four different types of distributions.

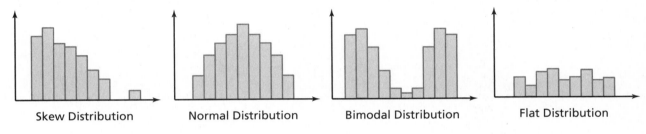

Skew Distribution   Normal Distribution   Bimodal Distribution   Flat Distribution

a. Describe a real-life example of each distribution.

b. Describe the mean, median, and mode of each distribution.

c. In which distributions are the mean and median about equal? Explain your reasoning.

d. How did each type of distribution get its name?

8.2 **Histograms** (continued)

2 **ACTIVITY:** Analyzing Distributions

Work with a partner. A survey asked 100 adult men and 100 adult women to answer the following questions.

> Question 1: What is your ideal weight?

> Question 2: What is your ideal age?

Match the histogram to the question.

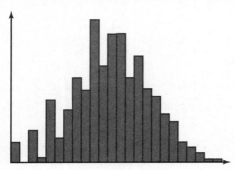

Graph for Question _____

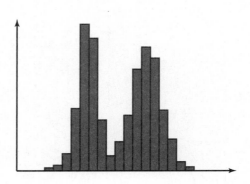

Graph for Question _____

3 **ACTIVITY:** Conducting Experiments

Work with a partner. Conduct two experiments. Make a frequency table and a histogram for each experiment. Compare and contrast the results of the two experiments.

> **a.** Toss *one* number cube 36 times. Record the numbers.

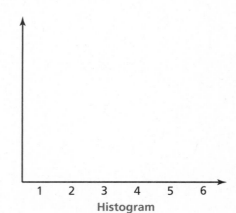

Frequency Table

Histogram

8.2 **Histograms** (continued)

   b. Toss *two* number cubes 36 times. Record the sums of the two numbers.

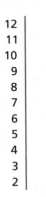

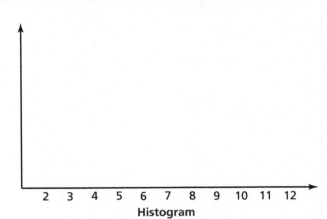

What Is Your Answer?

   4. **IN YOUR OWN WORDS** How do histograms show the differences in distributions of data?

   5. Describe an experiment that you can conduct to collect data. Predict the type of data distribution the results will create.

8.2 **Practice**
For use after Lesson 8.2

Display the data in a histogram.

1.

Birthdays	
Months	**Frequency**
Jan–Mar	15
Apr–June	9
Jul–Sept	6
Oct–Dec	12

2.

Goals Scored	
Goals	**Frequency**
0–2	6
3–5	8
6–8	2
9–11	1

3.

Height Jumped	
Inches	**Frequency**
0–11	7
12–23	10
24–35	5
36–47	2

4.

Money Spent	
Dollars	**Frequency**
0–19	3
20–39	8
40–59	8
60–79	15

5. The histogram shows the times students ran the mile in gym class.

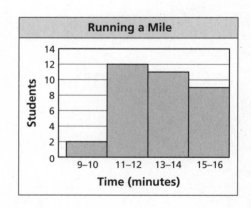

   a. Which interval contains the fewest data values?

   b. How many students are in the class?

   c. What percent of students ran the mile in 12 minutes or less?

Name_____ Date _____

Essential Question How can you use a circle graph to show the results of a survey?

1 ACTIVITY: Reading a Circle Graph

Work with a partner. Six hundred middle school students were asked "What is your favorite sport?" The circle graph shows the results of the survey.

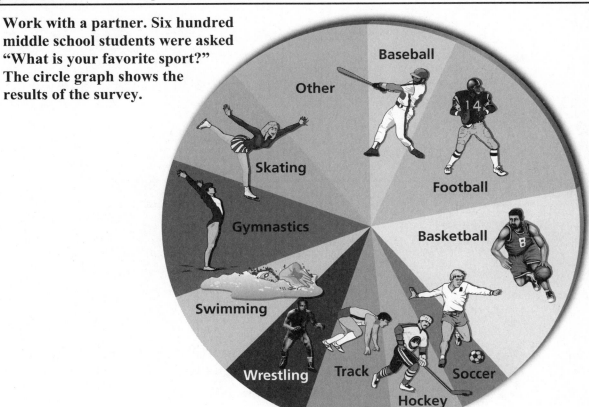

a. Use a protractor to find the angle measure (in degrees) of the section (pie piece) for football.

b. How many degrees are in a full circle?

8.3 **Circle Graphs** (continued)

   c. Write and solve a proportion to determine the number of students who said football is their favorite sport.

   d. Repeat the process for the other sections of the circle graph.

2 **ACTIVITY:** Making a Circle Graph

Work with a partner.

   a. Conduct a survey in your class. Each student should check his or her favorite sport on a piece of paper similar to the one shown below.

What is your favorite sport?			
Baseball	☐	Skating	☐
Basketball	☐	Soccer	☐
Football	☐	Swimming	☐
Gymnastics	☐	Track	☐
Hockey	☐	Wrestling	☐
		Other	☐

   b. Organize the results on the board.

   c. Display the results in a circle graph.

8.3 Circle Graphs (continued)

d. Compare and contrast your class survey with the survey in Activity 1.

What Is Your Answer?

3. **IN YOUR OWN WORDS** How can you use a circle graph to show the results of a survey?

4. Find a circle graph in a newspaper, in a magazine, or on the Internet. Copy it and describe the results that it shows.

"I conducted a survey and asked
30 people if they would like a
million dollars."

"I organized the results in a
circle graph."

8.3 Practice
For use after Lesson 8.3

Find the angle measure that corresponds to the percent of a circle.

1. 50%

2. 65%

3. 9%

Display the data in a circle graph.

4.

Toppings	Pizzas Ordered
Pepperoni	6
Sausage	6
Peppers	3
Extra Cheese	5

5.

Chore	Minutes
Vacuum	15
Dust	20
Make Bed	5
Wash Dishes	20

6. The circle graph shows the results from a class survey on favorite juice.

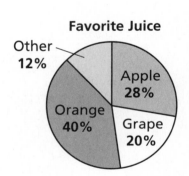

Favorite Juice

a. Compare the number of students who chose apple juice to the number of students who chose grape juice.

b. There are 25 students in the class. Find the number of students in each category.

8.4 Samples and Populations
For use with Activity 8.4

Essential Question   How can you use a survey to make conclusions about the general population?

1 ACTIVITY: Interpreting a Survey

Work with a partner. Read the newspaper article. Analyze the survey by answering the following questions.

a. The article does not say how many "teens and young adults" were surveyed. How many do you think need to be surveyed so that the results can represent all teens and young adults in your state? in the United States? Explain your reasoning.

The Daily Ti

VOL 01   No. 279   WEDNESDAY, OCTOBER 6, 2010

TEXT MESSAGING SURVEY RESULTS

A survey reports that almost one-third of teens and young adults believe that their text messaging plans are restrictive.

About 40% say their plans lead to higher cell phone bills. According to those participating in the survey, the average number of text messages sent per day is between 6 and 7.

The majority of survey participants say they would send more text messages if their cell phone plans were not as restrictive.

b. Outline the newspaper article. List all of the important points.

c. Write a questionnaire that could have been used for the survey. Do not include leading questions. For example, "Do you think your cell phone plan is restrictive?" is a leading question.

8.4 **Samples and Populations** (continued)

2 **ACTIVITY:** Conducting a Survey

Work with a partner. The newspaper article in Activity 1 states that the average number of text messages sent per day is between 6 and 7.

  a. Does this statement seem correct to you? Explain your reasoning.

  b. Plan a survey to check this statement. How will you conduct the survey?

  c. Survey your classmates. Organize your data using one of the types of graphs you have studied in this chapter.

  d. Write a newspaper article summarizing the results of your survey.

3 **ACTIVITY:** Conducting and Summarizing a Survey

Work with a partner.

 • Plan a survey to determine how many of the following texting shortcuts people know.

Texting Shortcuts			
R	Are	U	You
4	For	L8R	Later
SUP	What's up	TTYL	Talk to you later
PLZ	Please	BRB	Be right back
C	See	LOL	Laugh out loud
IDK	I don't know	BFF	Best friends forever
JK	Just kidding	THX	Thanks
2NITE	Tonight	GR8	Great
QPSA?	Que Pasa?	4COL	For crying out loud

8.4 **Samples and Populations** (continued)

- Write a questionnaire to use in your survey.

- In the survey, try to determine whether *teenagers* or *people over 30* know more of the short cuts.

- Conduct your survey. What can you conclude from the results? Do the results confirm your prediction?

What Is Your Answer?

4. IN YOUR OWN WORDS How can you use a survey to make conclusions about the general population?

5. Find a survey in a newspaper, in a magazine, or on the Internet. Decide whether you think the conclusion of the survey is correct. Explain your reasoning.

"I'm sending my Mom a text message for Mother's Day."

"2 GR8 2 ME 2 EVR B 4GOT10. XX00"

Name _____ Date _____

Identify the population and the sample.

1.

    Members of the   All sports players
    soccer team

2.

    8 crayons

    A box of crayons

Which sample is better for making a prediction? Explain.

3. Predict the average age of students in your school.
    Sample A: A random sample of 50 students in your school.
    Sample B: A random sample of 50 students in your class.

4. Predict the number of male dogs in the pet shop.
    Sample A: A random sample of 3 dogs in the pet shop.
    Sample B: A random sample of 15 dogs in the pet shop.

5. A survey asked 56 randomly chosen students if they play basketball. Seven
    said yes. There are 24 students who play basketball in your grade. Predict
    the number of students in your grade.

Chapter 9 Fair Game Review

Simplify the fraction.

1. $\dfrac{10}{12}$

2. $\dfrac{36}{72}$

3. $\dfrac{14}{28}$

4. $\dfrac{18}{26}$

5. $\dfrac{32}{48}$

6. $\dfrac{65}{91}$

7. There are 90 students involved in the mentoring program. Of these students, 60 are girls. Write and simplify a fraction showing the number of girls in the mentoring program.

8. There are 56 rows of vegetables planted in a field. Fourteen of the rows are corn. Write and simplify a fraction showing the number of rows of corn in the field.

Fair Game Review (continued)

Write the ratio in simplest form.

9. Bats to baseballs

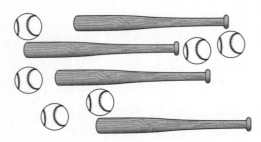

10. Bows to gift boxes

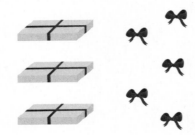

11. Hammers to screwdrivers

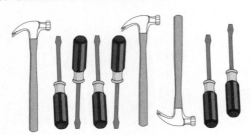

12. Apples to bananas

13. Flowers to vases

14. Cars to trucks

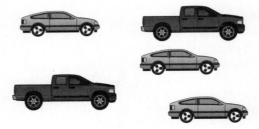

15. There are 100 students in the seventh grade. There are 15 seventh grade teachers. What is the ratio of teachers to students?

9.1 Introduction to Probability
For use with Activity 9.1

Essential Question How can you predict the results of spinning a spinner?

1 ACTIVITY: Helicopter Flight

Play with a partner.

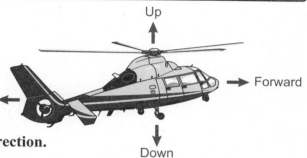

- You begin flying the helicopter at (0, 0) on the coordinate plane. Your goal is to reach the cabin at (20, 14).

- Spin any one of the spinners. Move one unit in the indicated direction.

- If the helicopter encounters any obstacles, you must start over.

- Record the number of moves it takes to land exactly on (20, 14).

- After you have played once, it is your partner's turn to play.

- The player who finishes in the fewest moves wins.

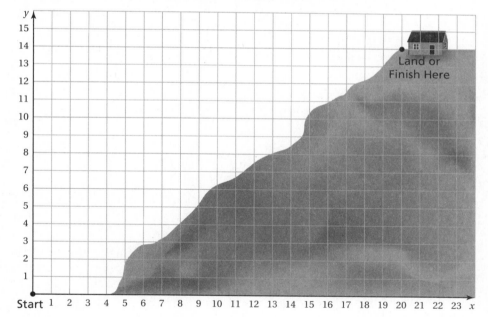

9.1 **Introduction to Probability** (continued)

2 **ACTIVITY:** Analyzing the Spinners

Work with a partner.

   a. How are the spinners in Activity 1 alike? How are they different?

   b. Which spinner will advance the helicopter to the finish faster? Why?

   c. If you want to move up, which spinner should you spin? Why?

   d. Spin each spinner 50 times and record the results.

Spinner A	
Up	
Down	
Reverse	
Forward	

Spinner B	
Up	
Down	
Reverse	
Forward	

Spinner C	
Up	
Down	
Reverse	
Forward	

Spinner D	
Up	
Down	
Reverse	
Forward	

9.1 **Introduction to Probability** (continued)

e. Organize the results from part (d) in a bar graph for each spinner.

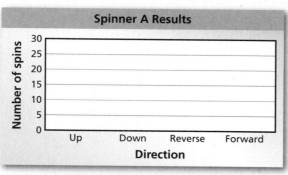

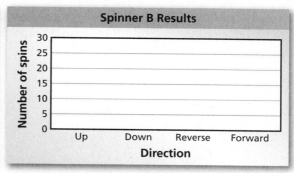

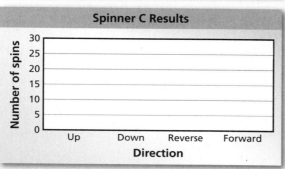

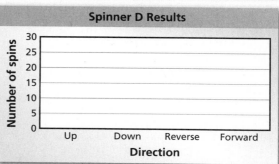

f. After analyzing the results, would you change your strategy in the helicopter flight game? Explain why or why not.

What Is Your Answer?

3. IN YOUR OWN WORDS How can you predict the results of spinning a spinner?

9.1 **Practice**
For use after Lesson 9.1

A bag is filled with 4 red marbles, 3 blue marbles, 3 yellow marbles, and 2 green marbles. You randomly choose one marble from the bag. (a) Find the number of ways the event can occur. (b) Find the favorable outcomes of the event.

1. Choosing red

2. Choosing green

3. Choosing yellow

4. Choosing *not* blue

5. In order to figure out who will go first in a game, your friend asks you to pick a number between 1 and 25.

   a. What are the possible outcomes?

   b. What are the favorable outcomes of choosing an even number?

   c. What are the favorable outcomes of choosing a number less than 20?

9.2 **Theoretical Probability**
For use with Activity 9.2

Essential Question   How can you find a theoretical probability?

1 **ACTIVITY:** Black and White Spinner Game

Work with a partner. You work for a game company. You need to create a game that uses the spinner below.

a. Write rules for a game that uses the spinner. Then play it.

b. After playing the game, do you want to revise the rules? Explain.

c. Each pie-shaped section of the spinner is the same size. What is the measure of the central angle of each section?

d. What is the probability that the spinner will land on 1? Explain.

9.2 **Theoretical Probability** (continued)

2 **ACTIVITY:** Changing the Spinner

Work with a partner. For each spinner, find the probability of landing on each number. Do your rules for Activity 1 make sense for these spinners? Explain.

a.

b.

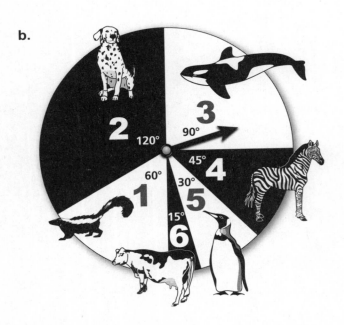

9.2 Theoretical Probability (continued)

3 ACTIVITY: Is This Game Fair?

Work with a partner. Apply the following rules to each spinner in Activities 1 and 2. Is the game fair? If not, who has the better chance of winning?

- **Take turns spinning the spinner.**

- **If the spinner lands on an odd number, Player 1 wins.**

- **If the spinner lands on an even number, Player 2 wins.**

What Is Your Answer?

4. IN YOUR OWN WORDS How can you find a theoretical probability?

5. Find and describe a career in which probability is used. Explain why probability is used in that career.

6. Two people play the following game.

Each player has 6 cards numbered 1, 2, 3, 4, 5, and 6. At the same time, each player holds up one card. If the product of the two numbers is odd, Player 1 wins. If the product is even, Player 2 wins. Continue until both players are out of cards. Which player is more likely to win? Why?

9.2 Practice
For use after Lesson 9.2

Use a number cube to determine the theoretical probability of the event.

1. Rolling a 2

2. Rolling a 5

3. Rolling an even number

4. Rolling a number greater than 1

A spinner is used for a game. Determine if the game is fair. If it is *not* fair, who has the greater probability of winning?

5. You win if the number is less than 4. If it is not less than 4, your friend wins.

6. You win if the number is a multiple of 2. If it is not a multiple of 2, your friend wins.

7. At a carnival, you pick a duck out of a pond that designates a prize. You want to win a large prize and the theoretical probability of winning it is $\frac{9}{25}$. There are 50 ducks. How many ducks will win a large prize?

9.3 Experimental Probability
For use with Activity 9.3

Essential Question What is meant by experimental probability?

1 ACTIVITY: Throwing Sticks

Play with a partner. This game is based on an Apache game called "Throw Sticks."

- **Take turns throwing three sticks into the center of the circle and moving around the circle according to the chart.**

- **If your opponent lands on or passes your playing piece, you must start over.**

- **The first player to pass his or her starting point wins.**

MOVE CHART

3 Decorated	10 stones
3 Plain	5 stones
2 Plain, 1 Decorated	3 stones
2 Decorated, 1 Plain	2 stones

Each stick has one plain side and one decorated side.

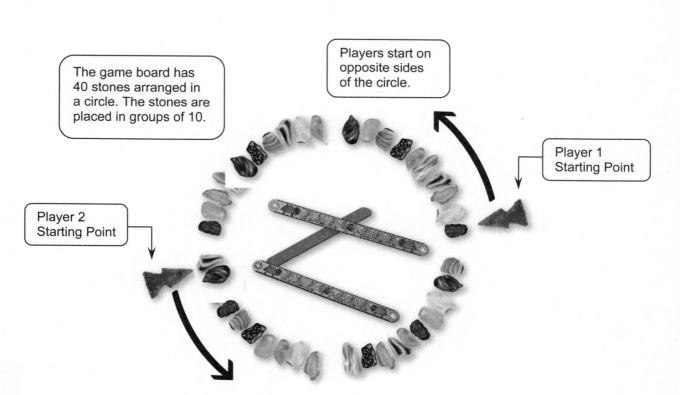

The game board has 40 stones arranged in a circle. The stones are placed in groups of 10.

Players start on opposite sides of the circle.

Player 1 Starting Point

Player 2 Starting Point

9.3 **Experimental Probability** (continued)

2 **ACTIVITY:** Conducting an Experiment

Work with a partner. Throw the 3 sticks 32 times. Tally the results using the outcomes listed below. A "P" represents the plain side landing up and a "D" represents the decorated side landing up. Organize the results in a bar graph. Use the bar graph to estimate the probability of each outcome. These are called experimental probabilities.

   a. PPP

   b. DPP

   c. DDP

   d. DDD

3 **ACTIVITY:** Analyzing the Possibilities

Work with a partner. A tree diagram helps you see different ways that the same outcome can occur.

   a. Find the number of ways that each outcome can occur.

     • Three Ps

     • One D and two Ps

     • Two Ds and one P

     • Three Ds

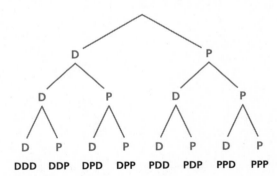

9.3 Experimental Probability (continued)

b. Find the theoretical probability of each outcome.

c. Compare and contrast your experimental and theoretical probabilities.

What Is Your Answer?

4. IN YOUR OWN WORDS What is meant by experimental probability?

5. Give a real-life example of experimental probability.

Name _____ Date _____

Use the bar graph to find the experimental probability.

1. Drawing red

2. Drawing orange

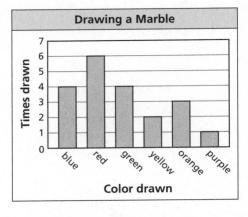

3. Drawing *not* yellow

4. Drawing a color with more than 4 letters in its name

5. There are 25 students' names in a hat. You choose 5 names. Three are boys' names and two are girls' names. How many of the 25 names would you expect to be boys' names?

6. You must stop at 3 of 5 stoplights on a stretch of road. If this trend continues, how many times will you stop if the road has 10 stoplights?

7. Your teacher has a large box containing an equal number of red and blue folders. There are 24 students in your class. The teacher passes out the folders at random. Ten students receive a red folder. Compare the experimental probability of receiving a red folder with the theoretical probability of receiving a red folder.

Name_____ Date _____

Essential Question What is the difference between dependent and independent events?

1 ACTIVITY: Dependent Events

Work with a partner. You have three marbles in a bag. There are two green marbles (G) and one purple marble (P). You randomly draw two marbles from the bag.

a. Use the tree diagram to find the probability that both marbles are green.

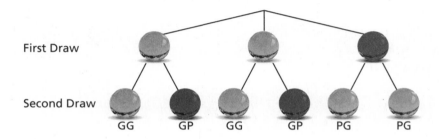

First Draw

Second Draw

GG   GP   GG   GP   PG   PG

b. In the tree diagram, does the probability of getting a green marble on the second draw *depend* on the color of the first marble? Explain.

2 ACTIVITY: Independent Events

Work with a partner. Using the same marbles from Activity 1, randomly draw a marble from the bag. Then put the marble back in the bag and draw a second marble.

a. Use the tree diagram to find the probability that both marbles are green.

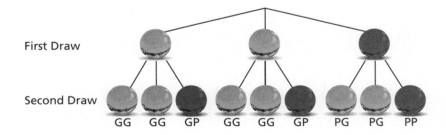

First Draw

Second Draw

GG GG GP GG GG GP PG PG PP

9.4   **Independent and Dependent Events** (continued)

b. In the tree diagram, does the probability of getting a green marble on the second draw *depend* on the color of the first marble? Explain.

3   **ACTIVITY:** Conducting an Experiment

Work with a partner. Conduct two experiments using two green marbles (G) and one purple marble (P).

a. In the first experiment, randomly draw two marbles from the bag 36 times. Record each result as GG or GP. Make a bar graph of your results.

GG	
GP	

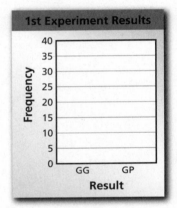

b. What is the experimental probability of drawing two green marbles? Does this answer seem reasonable? Explain.

9.4 **Independent and Dependent Events** (continued)

c. In the second experiment, randomly draw one marble from the bag. Put it back. Draw a second marble. Repeat this 36 times. Record each result as GG, GP, or PP. Make a bar graph of your results.

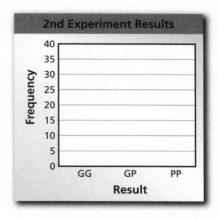

GG	
GP	
PP	

d. What is the experimental probability of drawing two green marbles? Does this answer seem reasonable? Explain.

What Is Your Answer?

4. IN YOUR OWN WORDS What is the difference between dependent and independent events? Describe a real-life example of each.

9.4 Practice
For use after Lesson 9.4

Tell whether the events are *independent* or *dependent*. Explain.

1. You spin a game spinner twice.
   First Spin: blue
   Second Spin: yellow

2. You roll a number cube twice
   First Roll: You roll a 6.
   Second Roll: You roll an odd number.

3. You and a friend are playing a game. You both randomly draw a playing piece and you get to draw first.
   Your Draw: red piece   Friend's Draw: blue piece

You roll a number cube twice. Use the tree diagram to find the probability of the events.

4. Rolling a 5 and then a 3

5. Rolling an even number on each roll

6. During a card trick, your friend asks you to pick two cards. A deck of cards has 52 cards and is divided evenly into four suits: hearts, diamonds, clubs, and spades. What is the probability that the first pick is a heart and the second is a diamond?

B.1 Solving Multi-Step Equations
For use with Activity B.1

Essential Question How can you convert temperatures between the Fahrenheit and Celsius scales?

1 ACTIVITY: Comparing Fahrenheit and Celsius

Work with a partner. The temperature scales show the relationship between the Fahrenheit and Celsius scales. Use the two scales to complete the table.

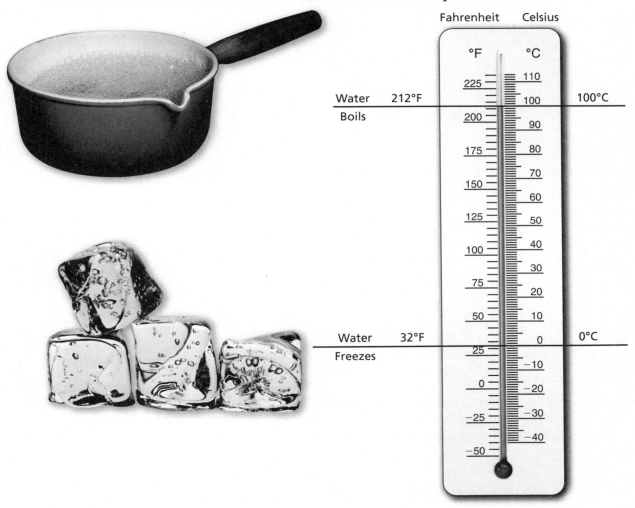

F	0°	32°	70°	80°	90°	100°	212°
C							

B.1   **Solving Multi-Step Equations** (continued)

2   **ACTIVITY:** Comparing Fahrenheit and Celsius

Work with a partner.

   a. Plot the points from the table in Activity 1.

   b. Draw a line through the points.

   c. Find the slope of the line. Write the slope as a fraction in simplest form.

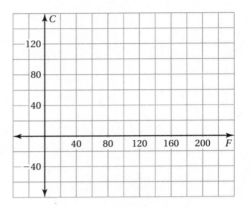

   d. Which of the following shows the relationship between C and F?

   $$C = \frac{5}{9}(F + 32)$$ $$C = \frac{5}{9}(F - 32)$$

   $$C = \frac{9}{5}(F + 32)$$ $$C = \frac{9}{5}(F - 32)$$

3   **ACTIVITY:** Converting Temperatures

Work with a partner. You have email pals in four countries that use the Celsius scale. Write each temperature in degrees Fahrenheit. Then use the scale in Activity 1 to check that your answer is reasonable.

   a. Canada: 19°C

B.1 **Solving Multi-Step Equations** (continued)

b. Mexico: 35°C

c. Japan: 28°C

d. Russia: 6°C

What Is Your Answer?

4. **IN YOUR OWN WORDS** How can you convert temperatures between the Fahrenheit and Celsius scales? Give two examples.

B.1 Practice
For use after Lesson B.1

Solve the equation. Check your solution.

1. $-2x + 8x = 9 + 3$

2. $-5w + 10w - 18 = 12$

3. $6k + 7 - 3k + 7k = 27$

4. $9(b - 2) + 1 = 19$

5. $4 + 5(c - 6) + 8c = -13$

6. $\dfrac{1}{2}(y - 18) = -2$

7. The length of a rectangular prism is 5 feet and its height is 6 feet. Find the width of the prism if the surface area is 126 square feet.

8. You receive x dollars an hour for babysitting. You babysit 3 hours on Friday and 5 hours on Saturday. You receive $40 for the two days. Write and solve an equation to find how much you earn per hour.

Name_____ Date _____

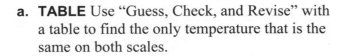

B.2 Solving Equations with Variables on Both Sides
For use with Activity B.2

Essential Question   How can you solve an equation that has variables on both sides?

---

1 **ACTIVITY:** Using a Table, Graph, and Algebra

Work with a partner. You have an email pal in Antarctica. Your email pal tells you the temperature in McMurdo. You ask whether he gave the temperature in Celsius or Fahrenheit. He says "It's the same on both scales." What is the temperature?

a. **TABLE** Use "Guess, Check, and Revise" with a table to find the only temperature that is the same on both scales.

F						
C						

b. **GRAPH** Draw the line given by $C = F$ in the coordinate plane. Locate the point at which the graph of $C = F$ intersects the graph of $C = \dfrac{5}{9}(F - 32)$.

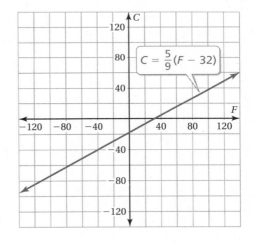

c. **ALGEBRA** Let x be the temperature that is the same on both scales.

Substitute x for C and F in the equation $C = \dfrac{5}{9}(F - 32)$. Then solve for x.

B.2 **Solving Equations with Variables on Both Sides** (continued)

d. Compare your solutions from parts (a)–(c). Did you get the same solution with each method? Which method do you prefer? Why?

2 **GAME:** Race to the South Pole

Play with a partner.

- Write each expression on a scrap of brown or blue paper. Place the brown pieces of paper in one bag and the blue pieces of paper in another bag.

- Draw an expression from each bag and set them equal to each other.

- If you can solve the equation, you move one space on the game board on the next page. If you cannot solve the equation, your partner gets a chance to solve it and move one space.

- Put the expressions back into their bags.

- Take turns. The first person to reach the South Pole wins.

Brown Papers	Blue Papers
x	$2x$
$x + 1$	$2x + 4$
$x - 1$	$-2x$
$x + 2$	$-2x + 4$
$x - 2$	$3x$
$x + 3$	$3x + 6$
$x - 3$	$-3x$
	$-3x + 6$

$$\boxed{x + 1} = \boxed{3x}$$

B.2 Solving Equations with Variables on Both Sides (continued)

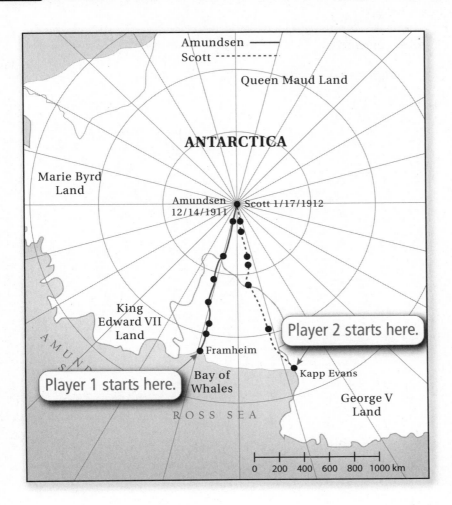

What Is Your Answer?

3. **IN YOUR OWN WORDS** How can you solve an equation that has variables on both sides? Give an example and solve it.

B.2 Practice
For use after Lesson B.2

Solve the equation. Check your solution.

1. $x = -2x - 21$

2. $-3x = 4x - 14$

3. $5p - 11 = 9p + 17$

4. $3.8d + 7 = -8.2d + 70$

5. $-7n + 6 = -3(3n + 10)$

6. $6(y - 5) = -2(5y - 1)$

7. You start a business making painted flower containers. You spend $300 on paint and $5 on each container. You charge $20 for each container. How many containers do you have to sell to break even?

8. There are 322 students in the seventh grade at your school. There are 48 more girls than boys. How many of each are in the seventh grade?

Name_____ Date _____

Essential Question How can you use tables and graphs to solve equations?

1 ACTIVITY: Using a Table, Graph, and Algebra

Work with a partner. You start a website design company. How many sites must you design before you start making a profit?

- **You pay $4000 for a new computer and software.**

- **It costs you $100 to design each website.**

- **You charge $500 to design each website.**

Let x represent the number of sites you design.

$C = 4000 + 100x$ Cost of designing x sites

$R = 500x$ Income for designing x sites

You will start making a profit when $C = R$. That is, when you have designed enough websites to cover your start-up cost of $4000 and $100 for each site.

a. TABLE Use "Guess, Check, and Revise" with a table to find the value of x for which $C = R$.

x							
C							
R							

b. GRAPH Graph $C = 4000 + 100x$ and $R = 500x$ in the same coordinate plane. Find the value of x for which the two lines intersect.

c. ALGEBRA Set C equal to R. Solve for x.

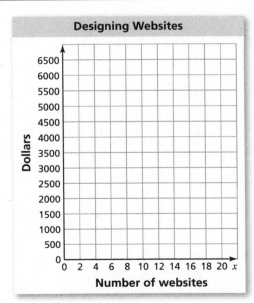

Designing Websites

B.3 Solving Equations Using Tables and Graphs (continued)

d. The point at which the two lines intersect is called the "break-even" point. Why is it called this?

---

2 **ACTIVITY:** Planning Your Own Business

Make a plan to start your own business.

- Describe your business.

- Are you providing a product or a service?

- Make a list of the things you need to start the business. Find the cost of each item or service.

- Write an equation that represents the cost of making x items. Write an equation that represents the income for selling x items.

B.3 **Solving Equations Using Tables and Graphs** (continued)

- Use a table to compare the cost and income for several values of *x*.

x							
C							
R							

- Draw a graph that shows when your company will reach the break-even point.

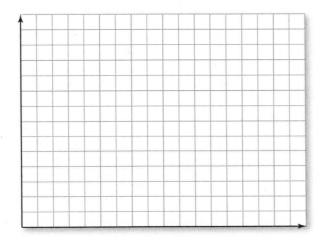

- Organize all of your planning in a folder. Include your company name, logo, and a plan for advertising and selling your product or service.

What Is Your Answer?

3. **IN YOUR OWN WORDS** How can you use tables and graphs to solve equations? Describe a real-life example.

B.3 **Practice**
For use after Lesson B.3

Use a table to solve the equation. Check your solution.

1. $2p + 8 = -2p$

2. $-4y - 7 = 10y$

3. $5p - 20 = 3p + 8$

4. $-6d + 15 = -10d - 9$

Use the graph to solve the equation. Check your solution.

5. $x + 2 = 2x + 1$

6. $4x - 4 = -2x + 2$

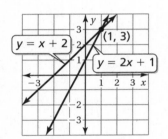

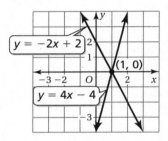

7. Company A sells a satellite radio for $300 and the music package for $10 per month. Company B sells a satellite radio for $200 and the music package for $15 per month.

    a. Use a graph to find the number of months it takes for the cost of Company A's products to equal the cost of Company B's products.

    b. If you are signing a two-year contract, which company should you buy from? Why?

Name_____ Date_____

Slope of a Line
For use with Activity B.4

Essential Question How can the slope of a line be used to describe the line?

You studied the following definition of the slope of a line.

Slope is the rate of change between any two points on a line. It is a measure of the *steepness* of a line. To find the slope of a line, find the ratio of the change in y (vertical change) to the change in x (horizontal change).

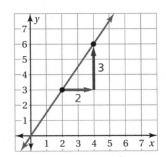

$$\textbf{slope} = \frac{\text{change in } y}{\text{change in } x}$$

$$= \frac{3}{2}$$

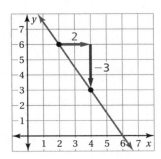

$$\textbf{slope} = \frac{\text{change in } y}{\text{change in } x}$$

$$= \frac{-3}{2} = -\frac{3}{2}$$

---

1   ACTIVITY: Extending the Concept of a Slope

Work with a partner. Find the slope of each line.

a.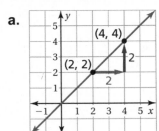

b.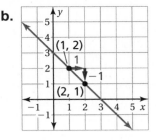

c.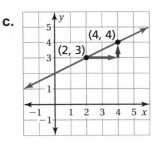

B.4 **Slope of a Line** (continued)

d.

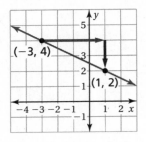

e.

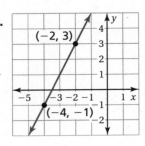

f.

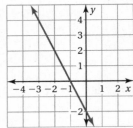

Inductive Reasoning

Work with a partner. Complete the table.

	Two Points	Change in *y*	Change in *x*	Slope of Line
1a	**2.** $(2, 2), (4, 4)$			
1b	**3.** $(1, 2), (2, 1)$			
1c	**4.** $(2, 3), (4, 4)$			
1d	**5.** $(-3, 4), (1, 2)$			
1e	**6.** $(-4, -1), (-2, 3)$			
1f	**7.**			
	8. $(-4, 0), (0, 1)$			
	9. $(-3, 4), (6, -2)$			
	10. $(-4, 2), (8, -1)$			
	11. $(-6, -1), (3, 5)$			
	12. $(-5, 7), (10, -5)$			
	13. $(0, 1), (4, 1)$			
	14. $(-4, -2), (-3, -6)$			

B.4 **Slope of a Line** (continued)

What Is Your Answer?

15. **IN YOUR OWN WORDS** How can the slope of a line be used to describe the line?

    a. Draw three lines that have positive slopes.

    b. Draw three lines that have negative slopes.

16. Compare a slope of 1 with a slope of 2. Show your comparison on a graph.

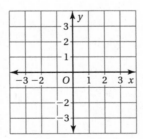

17. Compare a slope of −1 to a slope of −2. Show your comparison on a graph.

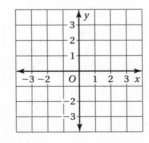

Name _____ Date _____

Find the slope of the line.

1.

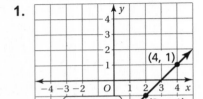

(4, 1)

$y = x - 3$ (2, −1)

2.

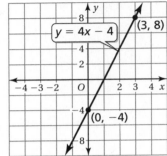

$y = 4x - 4$ (3, 8)

(0, −4)

Graph the line with the given slope that passes through the given point.

3. slope $= -1;\ (2, 3)$

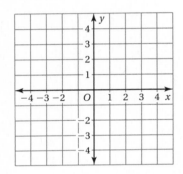

4. slope $= \dfrac{2}{3};\ (-1, 3)$

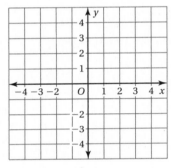

5. slope $= 4;\ (-2, -4)$

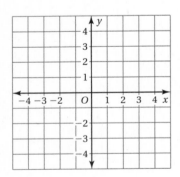

6. slope $= -\dfrac{1}{5};\ (3, -2)$

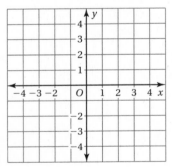

7. What is the slope of the ramp?

3 ft

8 ft

B.5 Linear Functions
For use with Activity B.5

Essential Question   How can you describe the graph of an equation of the form $y = mx + b$?

1   **ACTIVITY:** Using an Input-Output Table

Work with a partner.

a. Complete the input-output table for the equation $y = -\dfrac{1}{2}x + 2$.

Input, x	−3	−2	−1	0	1	2	3
Output, y							

b. Plot the points from the table.

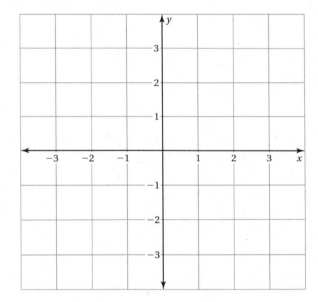

c. Describe the pattern of the points. Draw a graph that represents the pattern.

B.5 **Linear Functions** (continued)

    d. Choose three values of x that are not in the table. Find their corresponding y-values and plot the points on your graph from part (b). Do the points lie on the graph you made in part (c)?

Inductive Reasoning

Work with a partner. Sketch the graph of each equation. Then complete the table.

Equation	Description of Graph	Point of Intersection with y-axis	Slope of Graph
2. $y = -\dfrac{1}{2}x + 2$			
3. $y = -x + 2$			
4. $y = -x + 1$			
5. $y = -\dfrac{1}{2}x + 1$			
6. $y = x + 1$			
7. $y = x - 1$			
8. $y = \dfrac{1}{2}x - 1$			
9. $y = \dfrac{1}{2}x + 1$			
10. $y = 2x + 1$			
11. $y = 2x - 2$			
12. $y = -2x + 3$			

B.5 **Linear Functions** (continued)

What Is Your Answer?

13. **IN YOUR OWN WORDS** How can you describe the graph of an equation of the form $y = mx + b$?

    a. How does the value of m affect the graph?

    b. How does the value of b affect the graph?

    c. Test your answers to parts (a) and (b) with three equations that are not in the table.

14. Why is an equation of the form $y = mx + b$ called a linear function? What does the word *linear* mean? What does the word *function* mean?

B.5 Practice
For use after Lesson B.5

Find the slope and *y*-intercept of the graph of the linear function.

1. $y = \dfrac{5}{8}x - 6$
2. $y = -7x + 5$
3. $2x + 4y = 10$

Graph the linear function using slope-intercept form.

4. $y = 4x - 2$

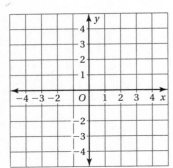

5. $3x + 5y = 20$

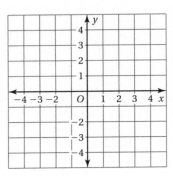

Write an equation of the linear function in slope-intercept form.

6.

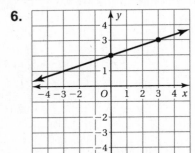

7.

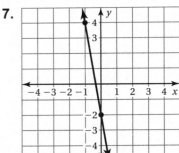

8. The number of songs *s* that you can learn to play on the piano after *n* weeks is given by $s = 8 + 3n$. What does the *y*-intercept represent? What does the slope represent?

Glossary

This student friendly glossary is designed to be a reference for key vocabulary, properties, and mathematical terms. Several of the entries include a short example to aid your understanding of important concepts.

Also available at BigIdeasMath.com:

- multi-language glossary
- vocabulary flash cards

---

absolute value

The distance between a number and 0 on a number line. The absolute value of a number a is written as $|a|$.

$$|-5| = 5$$
$$|5| = 5$$

acute angle

An angle whose measure is less than 90°.

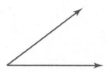

Addition Property of Equality

Adding the same number to each side of an equation produces an equivalent equation.

$$
\begin{array}{rcr}
x - 5 &=& -1 \\
+\,5 && +\,5 \\
\hline
x &=& 4
\end{array}
$$

additive inverse

The opposite of a number.

The additive inverse of 8 is −8.

Additive Inverse Property

The sum of an integer and its additive inverse is 0.

$$8 + (-8) = 0$$

angle

A figure formed by two rays with the same endpoint.

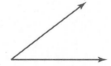

---

angle of rotation

The number of degrees a figure rotates.

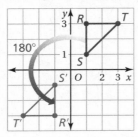

$\triangle RST$ has been rotated 180° to $\triangle R'S'T'$.

area

The amount of surface covered by a figure. Area is measured in square units such as square feet $\left(\text{ft}^2\right)$ or square meters $\left(\text{m}^2\right)$.

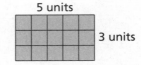

$A = 5 \times 3 = 15$ square units

bar graph

A graph in which the lengths of bars are used to represent and compare data.

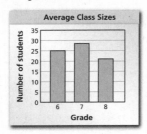

capacity

The amount a container can hold.

center of rotation

A fixed point about which a figure is rotated.

See rotation.

circle graph

Displays data sections of a circle. The circle represents all of the data. Each section represents part of the data. The sum of the angle measures in a circle graph is 360°.

circumference

The distance around a circle.

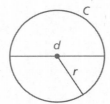

composite number

A whole number greater than 1 that has factors other than itself and 1.

12 is a composite number because the factors of 12 are 1, 2, 3, 4, 6, and 12.

composite solid	**cone**
A figure that is made up of more than one solid. 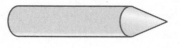	A solid that has one circular base and one vertex. 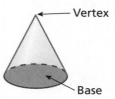

congruent	**congruent (figures)**
Having the same size and shape. 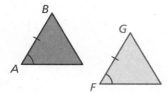 $\angle A$ is congruent to $\angle F$. Side AB is congruent to side FG.	Figures that have exactly the same size and shape. 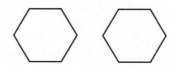

constant term	**coordinate plane**
A term that has a number but no variable. In the expression $2x + 8$, the term 8 is a constant term.	A coordinate plane is formed by the intersection of a horizontal number line, usually called the x-axis, and a vertical number line, usually called the y-axis. 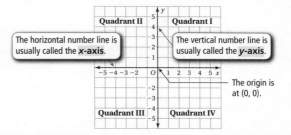

corresponding angles	**corresponding sides**
Matching angles of two similar figures. $\triangle ABC \sim \triangle DEF$ 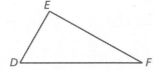 Corresponding angles: $\angle A$ and $\angle D$ $\angle B$ and $\angle E$ $\angle C$ and $\angle F$	Matching sides of two similar figures. $\triangle ABC \sim \triangle DEF$ 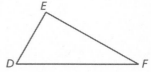 Corresponding sides: side AB and side DE side BC and side EF side AC and side DF

cross products

In the proportion $\dfrac{a}{b} = \dfrac{c}{d}$, where $b \neq 0$ and $d \neq 0$, the products $a \bullet d$ and $b \bullet c$ are called cross products.

$2 \bullet 6$ and $3 \bullet 4$

Cross Products Property

The cross products of a proportion are equal.

$2 \bullet 6 = 3 \bullet 4$

cube

A rectangular prism with 6 congruent square faces.

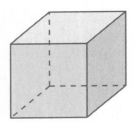

cube(d)

A number cubed is the number raised to the third power.

2 cubed means 2^3, or 8.

cylinder

A solid that has two parallel, congruent circular bases.

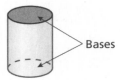

Bases

decimal

A number that is written using the base-ten place value system. Each place value is ten times the place value to the right.

The decimal 2.15 represents 2 ones plus 1 tenth plus 5 hundredths, or two and fifteen hundredths.

degree

A unit used to measure angles.

$90°, 45°, 32°$

denominator

The number below the fraction bar in a fraction.

In the fraction $\dfrac{2}{5}$, the denominator is 5.

dependent events

Two events such that the occurrence of one event affects the likelihood that the other event will occur.

A bag contains 3 red marbles and 4 blue marbles. You randomly draw a marble, do not replace it, then randomly draw another marble. The events "first marble is blue" and "second marble is red" are dependent events.

diameter (of a circle)

The distance across a circle through the center.

See circumference.

difference

The result when one number is subtracted from another number.

The difference of 4 and 3 is $4 - 3$, or 1.

dilation

A transformation in which a figure is enlarged or reduced.

direct variation

Two quantities x and y show direct variation when $y = kx$, where k is a number and $k \neq 0$.

The graph is a line that passes through the origin.

discount

A decrease in the original price of an item.

The original price for a pair of shoes is $95. The sale price is $65. The discount is $30.

Distributive Property

To multiply a sum or difference by a number, multiply each number in the sum or difference by the number outside the parentheses. Then evaluate.

$$3(2 + 9) = 3(2) + 3(9)$$
$$3(2 - 9) = 3(2) - 3(9)$$

Division Property of Equality

Dividing each side of an equation by the same number produces an equivalent equation.

$$-3y = 18$$
$$\frac{-3y}{-3} = \frac{18}{-3}$$
$$y = -6$$

equation

A mathematical sentence that uses an equal sign, =, to show that two expressions are equal.

$$4x = 16, a + 7 = 21$$

equivalent equation

Equations that have the same solution(s).

$$2x - 8 = 0 \text{ and } 2x = 8$$

estimate

To find an approximate solution to a problem.

You can estimate the sum of $98 + 53$ as $100 + 50$, or 150.

evaluate (an algebraic expression)

Substitute a number for each variable in an algebraic expression. Then use the order of operations to find the value of the numerical expression.

Evaluate $3x + 5$ when $x = 6$.
$$3x + 5 = 3(6) + 5$$
$$= 18 + 5$$
$$= 23$$

event

A collection of one or more favorable outcomes of an experiment.

Flipping heads on a coin.

experiment

An activity with varying results.

Rolling a number cube.

experimental probability

Probability that is based on repeated trials of an experiment.

$$P(\text{event}) = \frac{\text{number of times the event occurs}}{\text{total number of trials}}$$

A basketball player makes 19 baskets in 28 attempts. The experimental probability that the player makes a basket is $\frac{19}{28} = 68\%$.

expression

A mathematical phrase containing numbers, operations, and/or variables.

$$12 + 6, 18 + 3 \times 4$$
$$8 + x, 6 \times a - b$$

faces of a solid	**factor**
The polygons that form a solid figure.	When whole numbers other than zero are multiplied together, each number is a factor of the product.

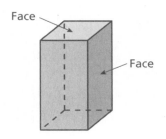

$2 \times 3 \times 4 = 24$, so 2, 3, and 4 are factors of 24.

---

fair experiment

An experiment in which all of the possible outcomes are equally likely.

The spinner is equally likely to land on 1 or 2. The spinner is fair.

The spinner is more likely to land on 1 than on either 2 or 3. The spinner is *not* fair.

favorable outcome

Outcomes corresponding to a specified event.

When rolling a number cube, the favorable outcomes for the event "rolling an even number" are 2, 4, and 6.

---

fraction

A number in the form $\frac{a}{b}$, where $b \neq 0$.

$$\frac{1}{2}, \frac{5}{9}$$

frequency table

A table used to count how many times data values occur in intervals.

Pairs of shoes	Frequency
1–5	11
6–10	4
11–15	0
16–20	3
21–25	6

---

frieze

A horizontal band that runs at the top of a building. A frieze is often decorated with a design that repeats.

Frieze

function

A relationship that pairs each input with exactly one output.

The ordered pairs $(0, 1)$, $(1, 2)$, $(2, 4)$, and $(3, 6)$ represent a function.

Ordered Pairs	Input	Output
$(0, 1)$	0	1
$(1, 2)$	1	2
$(2, 4)$	2	4
$(3, 6)$	3	6

greatest common factor (GCF) The largest of the common factors of two or more nonzero whole numbers. The common factors of 12 and 20 are 1, 2, and 4. So the GCF of 12 and 20 is 4.	**histogram** A bar graph that shows the frequency of data values in intervals of the same size. The height of a bar represents the frequency of the values in the interval. There are no spaces between bars. 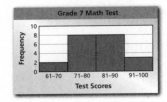
image The new figure formed by a transformation. *See translation, reflection, and rotation.*	**improper fraction** A fraction in which the numerator is greater than or equal to the denominator. $$\frac{5}{4}, \frac{9}{9}$$
independent events Two events such that the occurrence of one event does not affect the likelihood that the other event will occur. You flip a coin and roll a number cube. The events "flipping tails" and "rolling a 4" are independent events	**indirect measurement** Using similar figures to find a missing measurement that is difficult to find directly. 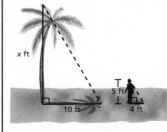 $$\frac{x}{10} = \frac{5}{4}$$ $$10 \bullet \frac{x}{10} = 10 \bullet \frac{5}{4}$$ $$x = 12.5$$ The tree is 12.5 feet tall.
input A number on which a function operates. *See function.*	**integers** The set of whole numbers and their opposites. $$\dots -3, -2, -1, 0, 1, 2, 3, \dots$$

interest	**inverse operations**
Money paid or earned for the use of money. *See simple interest.*	Operations that "undo" each other, such as addition and subtraction or multiplication and division.

inverse variation	**isosceles triangle**
Two quantities x and y show inverse variation when $y = \dfrac{k}{x}$, where k is a number and $k \neq 0$. The graph is not a line. 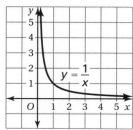	A triangle that has at least two congruent sides. 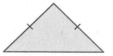

lateral edge of a prism	**lateral face**
The segments connecting the corresponding vertices of the bases of a prism. 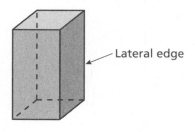	Any face or surface that is not a base. 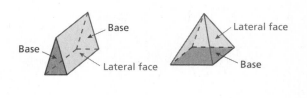

lateral surface area	**leaf**
The surface area of a figure excluding the area of its base(s). 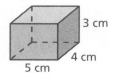 Lateral surface area $= 2(4)(3) + 2(5)(3)$ $\qquad\qquad\qquad = 24 + 30 = 54 \text{ cm}^2$	Digit or digits on the right of a stem-and-leaf plot. *See stem-and-leaf plot.*

least common denominator (LCD)	least common multiple (LCM)
The least common multiple of the denominators of two or more fractions. The least common denominator of $\frac{3}{4}$ and $\frac{5}{6}$ is the least common multiple of 4 and 6, or 12.	The smallest of the common multiples of two or more nonzero whole numbers. Multiples of 10: 10, 20, 30, 40, … Multiples of 15: 15, 30, 45, 60, … The least common multiple of 10 and 15 is 30.
like terms Terms that have identical variable parts. 4 and 8, $2x$ and $7x$	**line** A set of points that extends without end in two opposite directions. 
line graph A type of graph in which points representing data pairs are connected by line segments. 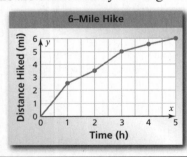	**line of reflection** A line that a figure is flipped across to create a mirror image of the original figure. *See reflection.*
line segment Part of a line that consists of two points, called endpoints, and all of the points on the line between the endpoints.	**linear function** A function whose graph is a line. $y = x - 1$ 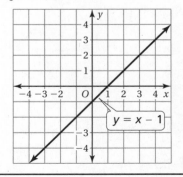

markup

An increase from the original cost to the selling price.

A store buys a hat for $12 and sells it for $20. The markup is $8.

mean

The sum of the values in a data set divided by the number of data values.

The mean of the values 7, 4, 8, and 9 is

$$\frac{7 + 4 + 8 + 9}{4} = \frac{28}{4} = 7.$$

median

For a data set with an odd number of ordered values, the median is the middle data value. For a data set with an even number of ordered values, the median is the mean of the two middle values.

The median of the data set 24, 25, 29, 33, 38 is 29 because 29 is the middle value.

metric system

Decimal system of measurement, based on powers of 10, that contains units for length, capacity, and mass.

centimeter, meter, liter, kilogram

mixed number

A number that has a whole number part and a fraction part.

$$3\frac{1}{2}, \ 6\frac{2}{3}$$

mode

The data value or values that occur most often. Data can have one mode, more than one mode, or no mode.

The modes of the data set 3, 4, 4, 7, 7, 9, 12 are 4 and 7 because they occur most often.

Multiplication Property of Equality

Multiplying each side of an equation by the same number produces an equivalent equation.

$$\frac{x}{3} = -6$$

$$3 \bullet \frac{x}{3} = 3 \bullet (-6)$$

$$x = -18$$

negative number

A number less than 0.

$$-0.25, -10, -500$$

net

A two-dimensional representation of a solid.

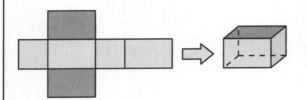

number line

A line whose points are associated with numbers that increase from left to right.

numerator

The number above the fraction bar in a fraction.

In the fraction $\dfrac{2}{5}$, the numerator is 2.

numerical expression

An expression that contains only numbers and operations.

$$12 + 6, 18 + 3 \times 4$$

oblique cone

A cone that *does not* have its vertex aligned directly above the center of its base.

oblique cylinder

A cylinder that *does not* have one base aligned directly above the other.

obtuse angle

An angle whose measure is greater than 90° and less than 180°.

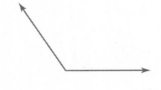

opposites

Two numbers that are the same distance from 0, but on opposite sides of 0.

−3 and 3 are opposites.

ordered pair A pair of numbers (x, y) used to locate a point in a coordinate plane. The first number is the x-coordinate, and the second number is the y-coordinate. The x-coordinate of the point $(-2, 1)$ is -2, and the y-coordinate is 1.	**origin** The point, represented by the ordered pair (0, 0), where the x-axis and the y-axis meet in a coordinate plane. *See coordinate plane.*
outcome A possible result of an experiment. The outcomes of flipping a coin are heads and tails.	**outlier** A data value that is much greater or much less than the other values. In the data set 23, 42, 33, 117, 36, and 40, the outlier is 117.
output A number produced by evaluating a function using a given input. *See function.*	**parallel (lines)** Two lines in the same plane that do not intersect. 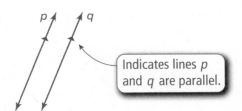 Indicates lines p and q are parallel.
parallelogram A quadrilateral with two pairs of parallel sides. 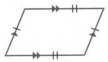	**percent** A ratio whose denominator is 100. The symbol for percent is %. $$40\% = \frac{40}{100} = 0.4$$

percent equation	**percent of change**
To represent "*a* is what percent of *w*," use the equation $a = p \cdot w$. 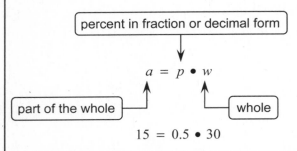 $$15 = 0.5 \cdot 30$$	The percent that a quantity changes from the original amount. $$\text{percent of change} = \frac{\text{amount of change}}{\text{original amount}}$$ The percent of change from 20 to 25 is: $$\frac{25 - 20}{20} = \frac{5}{20} = 25\%$$
percent of decrease	**percent of increase**
The percent of change when the original amount decreases. percent of decrease $$= \frac{\text{original amount} - \text{new amount}}{\text{original amount}}$$ The price of a shirt decreases from \$20 to \$10. The percent of decrease is $\frac{20 - 10}{20}$, or 50%.	The percent of change when the original amount increases. percent of increase $$= \frac{\text{new amount} - \text{original amount}}{\text{original amount}}$$ The price of a shirt increases from \$20 to \$30. The percent of increase is $\frac{30 - 20}{20}$, or 50%.
perimeter	**pi** (π)
The distance around a figure. Perimeter is measured in linear units such as feet (ft) or meters (m). 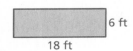 Perimeter = 18 + 6 + 18 + 6 = 48 ft	The ratio of the circumference of a circle to its diameter. You can use 3.14 or $\frac{22}{7}$ to approximate π.
place value	**point**
The place value of each digit in a number depends on its position within the number. In 521, 5 is in the hundreds place and has a value of 500.	A position in space represented with a dot.

polygon

A closed plane figure made up of three or more line segments that intersect only at their endpoints.

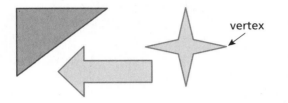

vertex

polyhedron

A three-dimensional figure whose faces are all polygons.

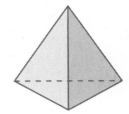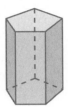

population

An entire group of people or objects.

All of the students in a school are a population. All of the students in a class are a sample of that population.

positive number

A number greater than 0.

0.5, 2, 100

power

A product formed from repeated multiplication by the same number or expression. A power consists of a base and an exponent.

$$2^4 = 2 \bullet 2 \bullet 2 \bullet 2 = 16$$

principal

An amount of money borrowed or deposited.

See simple interest.

prism

A polyhedron that has two parallel, congruent bases. The other faces are parallelograms.

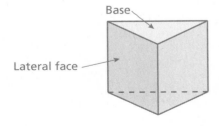

Base

Lateral face

probability

A number from 0 to 1 that measures the likelihood that an event will occur.

See experimental probability and theoretical probability.

product

The result when two or more numbers are multiplied.

The product of 4 and 3 is 4×3, or 12.

proportion

An equation stating that two ratios are equivalent.

$$\frac{3}{4} = \frac{12}{16}$$

proportional

Two quantities that form a proportion are proportional.

Because $\frac{3}{4}$ and $\frac{12}{16}$ form a proportion,

$\frac{3}{4}$ and $\frac{12}{16}$ are proportional.

protractor

A tool used to measure angles.

pyramid

A polyhedron that has one base. The other faces are triangles.

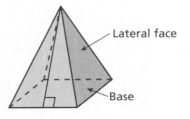

Lateral face

Base

quadrants

The four regions created by the intersection of the x-axis and the y-axis in a coordinate plane.

See coordinate plane.

quadrilateral

A polygon with four sides.

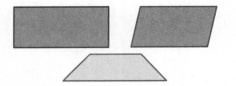

quotient

The result of a division.

The quotient of 10 and 5 is $10 \div 5$, or 2.

radius (of a circle)

The distance from the center of a circle to any point on the circle.

See circumference.

random sample

A sample in which each member of the population has an equal chance of being selected.

For the population at a school, a random sample would be every 10th student that arrives at school in the morning.

---

range (of a data set)

The difference between the greatest value and the least value of a data set. The range describes how spread out the data are.

The range of the data set 12, 16, 18, 22, 27, 35 is $35 - 12 = 23$.

rate

A ratio of two quantities with different units.

You read 3 books every 2 weeks.

---

ratio

A comparison of two quantities using division. The ratio of a to b (where $b \neq 0$) can be written as a to b, $a : b$, or $\dfrac{a}{b}$.

$$4 \text{ to } 1, \ 4 : 1, \text{ or } \dfrac{4}{1}$$

rational number

A number that can be written as the ratio of two integers, $\dfrac{a}{b}$, where a and b are integers and $b \neq 0$.

$$3 = \dfrac{3}{1}, \qquad\qquad -\dfrac{2}{5} = \dfrac{-2}{5}$$

$$0.25 = \dfrac{1}{4}, \qquad\qquad 1\dfrac{1}{3} = \dfrac{4}{3}$$

---

ray

A part of a line that has one endpoint and extends without end in one direction.

reciprocals

Two numbers whose product is 1.

Because $\dfrac{4}{5} \times \dfrac{5}{4} = 1$, $\dfrac{4}{5}$ and $\dfrac{5}{4}$ are reciprocals.

---

rectangle

A parallelogram with four right angles.

reflection

A transformation in which a figure flips over a line called the line of reflection. A reflection creates a mirror image of the original figure.

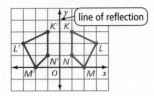

$K'L'M'N'$ is a reflection of $KLMN$ over the y-axis.

regular polygon

A polygon with congruent sides and congruent angles.

regular pyramid

A pyramid whose base is a regular polygon.

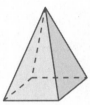

remainder

If a divisor does not divide a dividend evenly, the remainder is the whole number left over after the division.

$$\begin{array}{r} 4 \ \ \text{R}\,2 \\ 7\overline{)30} \\ \underline{28} \\ 2 \end{array}$$ The remainder is 2.

repeating decimal

A decimal that has a pattern that repeats.

$$0.555.. = 0.\overline{5}$$
$$1.727272... = 1.\overline{72}$$

rhombus

A parallelogram with four sides of equal length.

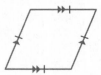

right angle

An angle whose measure is 90°.

rise The change in y between two points on a line. *See slope.*	**rotation** A transformation in which a figure turns around a point called the center of rotation. 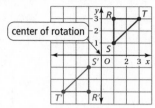 $\triangle RST$ has been rotated about the origin O to $\triangle R'S'T'$.
rotational symmetry A figure has rotational symmetry if a turn of 180° or less produces an image that fits exactly on the original figure. The figure has 60° rotational symmetry.	**round** To approximate a number to a given place value. 132 rounded to the nearest ten is 130.
run The change in x between two points on a line. *See slope.*	**sales tax** An additional amount of money charged on items by governments to raise money. A 6% sales tax on a \$20 item is $\$20 \times 0.06 = \$1.20$.
sample A part of a population. *See population.*	**scale** A ratio that compares the measurements of a drawing or model to the actual measurements. 12 cm : 1 cm 2 in. : 15 ft

scale drawing

A proportional two-dimensional drawing of an object.

A blueprint or a map

scale factor

A scale without units.

See ratio.

scale model

A proportional three-dimensional model of an object.

similar figures

Figures that have the same shape but not necessarily the same size.

Two figures are similar if corresponding side lengths are proportional, and corresponding angles have the same measure.

similar solids

Solids of the same type that have proportional corresponding linear measures.

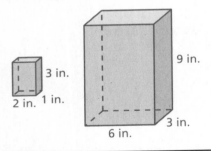

simple interest

Money paid or earned only on the principal.

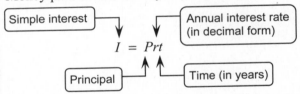

$$I = Prt$$

You put $200 into an account. The account earns 5% simple interest per year. The interest earned after 3 years is $200 × 0.05 × 3, or $30. The account balance is $200 + $30 = $230 after 3 years.

simplest form of a fraction

A fraction is in simplest form if its numerator and denominator have a greatest common factor (GCF) of 1.

The simplest form of the fraction $\frac{10}{15}$ is $\frac{2}{3}$.

slant height (of a cone)

The distance from the vertex of a cone to any point on the edge of its base.

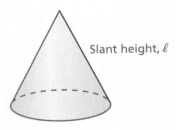

Slant height, ℓ

slant height (of a pyramid)	**slope**
The height of each triangular face of a pyramid. 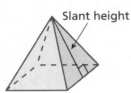	A ratio of the change in y (the rise) to the change in x (the run) between any two points on a line. It is a measure of the steepness of a line. $$\text{slope} = \frac{\text{change in } y}{\text{change in } x} = \frac{\text{rise}}{\text{run}}$$
slope-intercept form	**solid**
A linear function written in the form $y = mx + b$. The slope of the line is m and the y-intercept of the line is b. The slope is 1 and the y-intercept is 2.	A three-dimensional figure. *See three-dimensional figure.*
solution (of an equation)	**square**
A value that makes an equation true. 6 is the solution of the equation $x - 4 = 2$.	A parallelogram with four right angles and four sides of equal length.
square(d)	**stem**
A number squared is the number raised to the second power. 5 squared means 5^2, or 25.	Digit or digits on the left of a stem-and-leaf plot. *See stem-and-leaf plot.*

stem-and-leaf plot A type of data display that uses the digits of data values to organize a data set. Each data value is broken into a stem (digit or digits on the left) and a leaf (digit or digits on the right).	**straight angle** An angle whose measure is 180°. 

Test Scores

Stem	Leaf
6	6
7	2 7
8	1 1 3 4 4 6 8 8
9	0 0 0 2 7 8
10	0

Key: 9 | 4 = 94 points

Subtraction Property of Equality Subtracting the same number from each side of an equation produces an equivalent equation. $$\begin{aligned} w + 5 &= 25 \\ -5 & -5 \\ x &= 20 \end{aligned}$$	**sum** The result when two or more numbers are added. The sum of 4 and 3 is $4 + 3$, or 7.

surface area (of a prism) The sum of the areas of all the faces of a prism. $$\begin{aligned} S &= 2\ell w + 2\ell h + 2wh \\ &= 2(3)(5) + 2(3)(6) + 2(5)(6) \\ &= 30 + 36 + 60 \\ &= 126 \text{ in.} \end{aligned}$$ 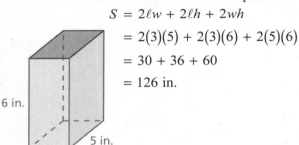 6 in. 5 in. 3 in.	**surface area of a polyhedron** The sum of the areas of the faces of a polyhedron. 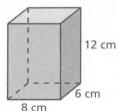 12 cm 6 cm 8 cm Surface area $= 2(8)(12) + 2(8)(6) + 2(12)(6)$ $= 432 \text{ cm}^2$

terminating decimal A decimal that ends. $1.5, \; 2.58, \; -5.605$	**terms** The parts of an expression that are added together. The terms of $4x + 7$ are $4x$ and 7.

tessellation

A repeating pattern of congruent plane figures that completely covers a plane with no holes or overlaps.

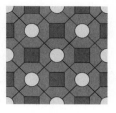

theoretical probability

The ratio of the number of favorable outcomes to the number of possible outcomes when all possible outcomes are equally likely.

$$P(\text{event}) = \frac{\text{number of favorable outcomes}}{\text{number of possible outcomes}}$$

When rolling a number cube, the theoretical probability of rolling a 4 is $\frac{1}{6}$.

three-dimensional figure

A figure that has length, width, and depth; also known as a solid.

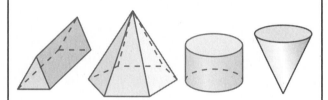

transformation

Changing a figure into another figure.

See translation, reflection, and rotation.

translation

A transformation in which a figure slides but does not turn. Every point of the figure moves the same distance and in the same direction.

trapezoid

A quadrilateral with exactly one pair of parallel sides.

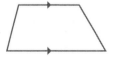

tree diagram

A branching diagram that shows all possible outcomes in a probability experiment.

All possible outcomes of tossing a coin three times.

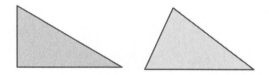

triangle

A polygon with three sides.

two-dimensional figure A figure that has only length and width. 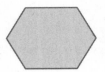	**U.S. customary system** System of measurement that contains units for length, capacity, and weight. inches, feet, quarts, gallons, ounces, pounds
unit rate A rate with a denominator of 1. The speed limit is 65 miles per hour.	**variable** A symbol, usually a letter, that represents one or more numbers. x is a variable in $2x + 1$.
variable term A term that has a variable. In the expression $2x + 8$, the term $2x$ is a variable term.	**vertex of a polygon** A point at which two sides of a polygon meet. The plural of vertex is vertices. *See polygon.*
vertex of a solid A point where the edges of a solid meet. The plural of vertex is vertices. 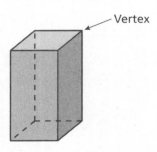	**volume** A measure of the amount of space that a three-dimensional figure occupies. Volume is measured in cubic units such as cubic feet (ft^3) or cubic meters (m^3). 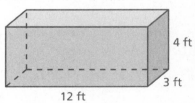 Volume $= 12 \cdot 3 \cdot 4 = 144 \text{ ft}^3$

whole numbers The numbers $0, 1, 2, 3, 4, \ldots$	***x*-axis** The horizontal number line in a coordinate plane. *See coordinate plane.*
***x*-coordinate** The first coordinate in an ordered pair, which indicates how many units to move to the left or right. In the ordered pair $(3, 5)$, the *x*-coordinate is 3.	***y*-axis** The vertical number line in a coordinate plane. *See coordinate plane.*
***y*-coordinate** The second coordinate in an ordered pair, which indicates how many units to move up or down. In the ordered pair $(3, 5)$, the *y*-coordinate is 5.	***y*-intercept** The *y*-coordinate of the point where a line crosses the *y*-axis. *See slope-intercept form.*

Photo Credits

72 Jean Thompson; 79 Baldwin Online; Children's
Literature Project; 107 *top* ©iStockphoto.com/
Viatcheslav Dusaleev; *bottom left* ©iStockphoto.com/
Jason Mooy; *bottom center* ©iStockphoto.com/Andres
Peiro Palmer; *bottom right* ©iStockphoto.com/
Felix Möckel; 139 *bottom left www.cartoonstock.com*;
bottom right M.C. Escher's, Ascending and Descending
©2008 The M.C. Escher Company-Holland. All
rights reserved. *www.mcescher.com*; 149 *bottom row
1 left* ©iStockphoto.com/Luke Daniek; *bottom row
1 right* ©iStockphoto.com/Jeff Whyte; *bottom row
2 left* ©Michael Mattox/BigStockPhoto.com; *bottom row
2 right* ©iStockphoto.com/Hedda Gjerpen;
219 ©iStockphoto.com/sweetym; 410 ©iStockphoto.com/
Wojciech Krusinski

Cartoon Illustrations Tyler Stout

a.   b.   c.   d.

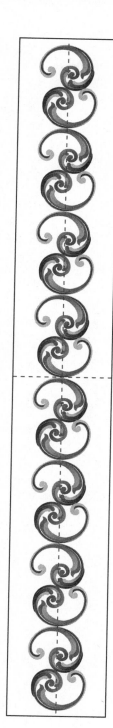

For use with Chapter 5 Section 7

For use with Chapter 6 Section 2 Activity 1

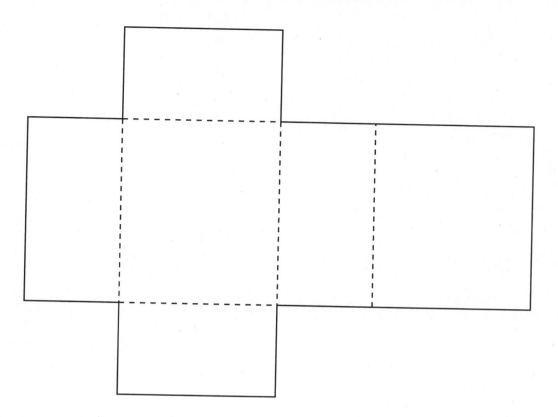

For use with Chapter 6 Section 2 Activity 2

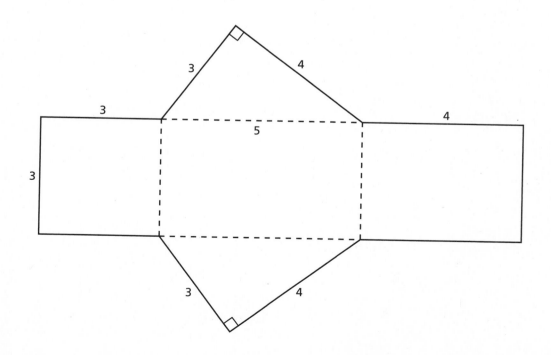

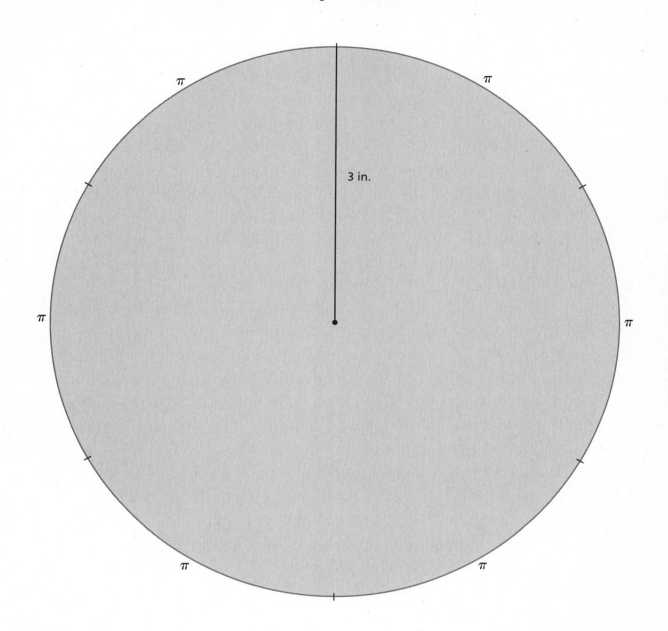

3 in.

1.25	0.75	$\dfrac{3}{4}$	0.6
-0.6	$\dfrac{19}{10}$	-0.4	$-\dfrac{2}{5}$
$-\dfrac{3}{4}$	-1.2	-0.75	1.6
$\dfrac{3}{10}$	$\dfrac{8}{5}$	1.9	$-\dfrac{3}{10}$
$-\dfrac{3}{2}$	$\dfrac{3}{20}$	1.5	$\dfrac{6}{5}$

-0.3	0.3	$-\dfrac{19}{10}$	$-\dfrac{8}{5}$
-1.6	1.2	$-\dfrac{3}{20}$	0.4
$\dfrac{3}{5}$	$-\dfrac{3}{5}$	$\dfrac{2}{5}$	-1.25
$\dfrac{5}{4}$	$-\dfrac{6}{5}$	-1.9	$\dfrac{3}{2}$
-0.15	-1.5	$-\dfrac{5}{4}$	0.15

$-9 = 9x$	$x = -6$	$-1 = x + 5$	$x = 3$
$2x = -10$	$\dfrac{x}{-2} = -2$	$x - 2 = 1$	$-8 = -2x$
$x - 3 = 1$	$-3x = -3$	$-7x = -14$	$\dfrac{x}{3} = -1$
$x - 1 = 1$	$x = -2$	$-3x = -9$	$9x = -27$
$-4x = -12$	$3 + x = -2$	$6x = -36$	$x = -1$

$-2 = -3 + x$	$x + 13 = 11$	$-4 + x = -2$	$x - 5 = -4$
$x = -4$	$x = 2$	$\dfrac{x}{2} = -2$	$x + 6 = 2$
$-10 = 10x$	$-16 = 8x$	$x = 1$	$x = 4$
$-7 = -1 + x$ $\quad x = -5$	$x + 9 = 8$	$-8 = 2x$	$-6 = x - 3$
$-20 = 10x$	$x = -3$	$\dfrac{x}{5} = -1$	

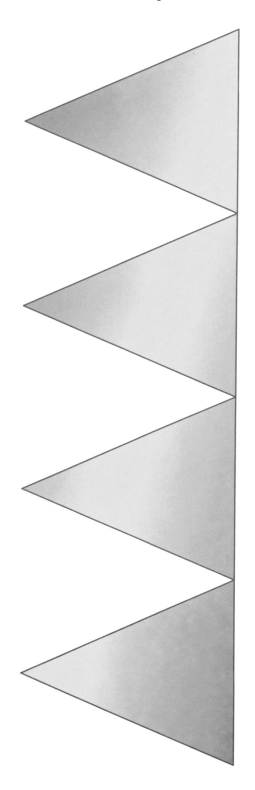

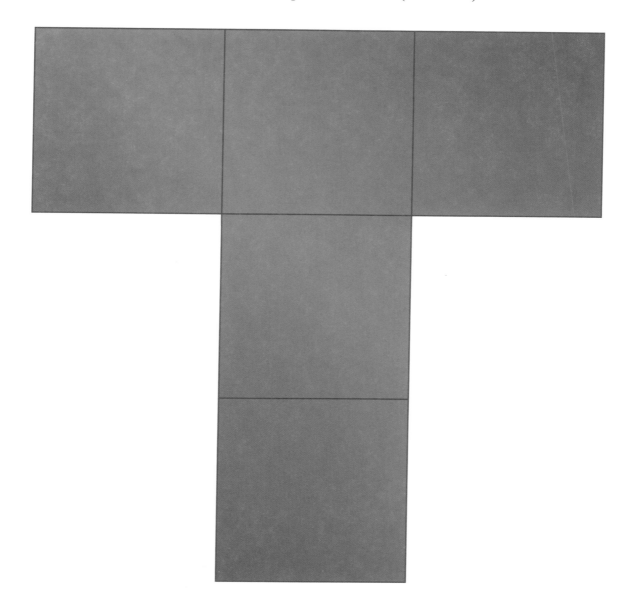

Integer Counters

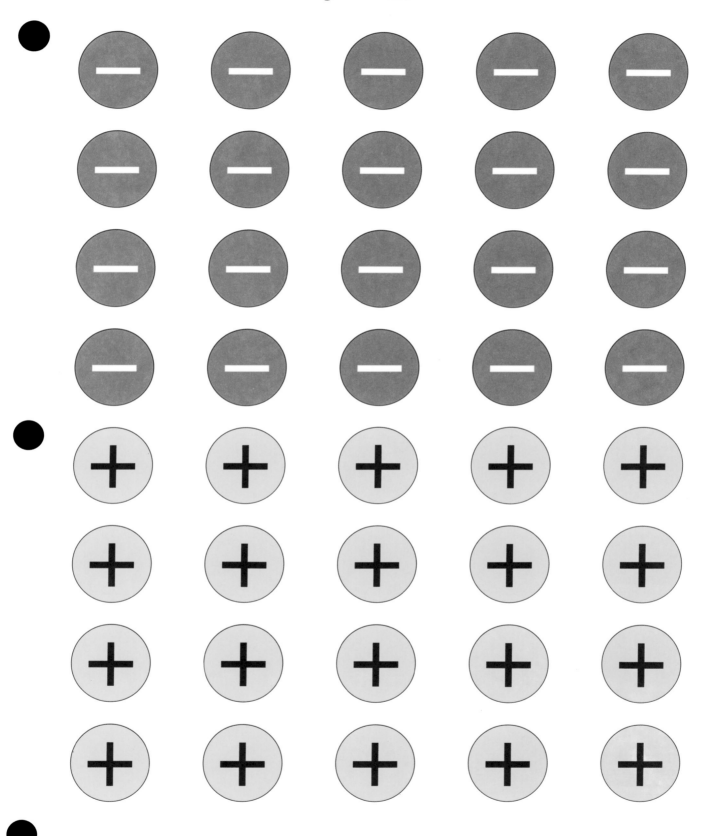

Algebra Tiles

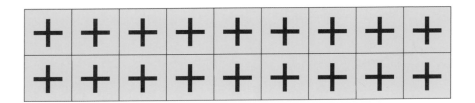

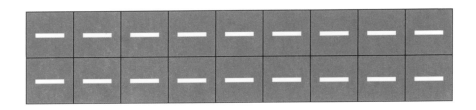

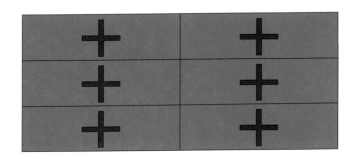

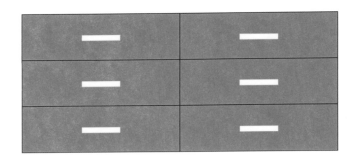

Algebra Tiles

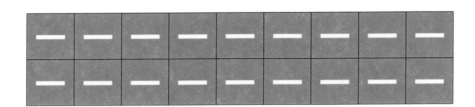

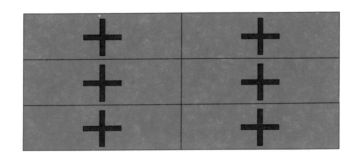

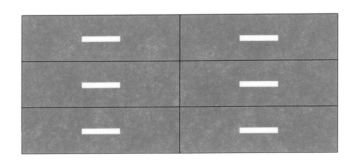

Pattern Blocks